# Cambridge Plain Texts

# SPENSER

## THE SHEPHEARDS CALENDER

T0346152

# SPENSER

## THE SHEPHEARDS CALENDER

CAMBRIDGE
AT THE UNIVERSITY PRESS
1923

CAMBRIDGE UNIVERSITY PRESS
Cambridge, New York, Melbourne, Madrid, Cape Town,
Singapore, São Paulo, Delhi, Mexico City

Cambridge University Press
The Edinburgh Building, Cambridge CB2 8RU, UK

Published in the United States of America by Cambridge University Press, New York

www.cambridge.org
Information on this title: www.cambridge.org/9781107669116

First published 1923
Re-issued 2013

*A catalogue record for this publication is available from the British Library*

ISBN 978-1-107-66911-6 Paperback

# NOTE

*The Shepheards Calender* was published in 1579 over the pseudonym of *Immerito*. The authorship was but thinly concealed; the preface addressed to Gabriel Harvey and signed with the initials of Edward Kirke gave hint enough that Colin Clout, his friend Hobbinol and his learned commentator had met, not in Arcady, but at Pembroke Hall, Cambridge. *Immerito* was soon identified with Edmund Spenser.

This book, so modestly put forth, won for Spenser the title of "the new poet"; his friends claimed, and most critics conceded, that he had given fresh inspiration to native English poetry at a moment when it seemed in danger of being sterilised by too much absorption of foreign and classical influence. Sidney, to whom the book was dedicated, might question Spenser's "forming his stile to an old rustick language," but this archaism drew men back to Spenser's model, his *Tityrus*, our English Chaucer.

Some of the fascination of this book for the Elizabethans has no doubt faded; the charm of the pastoral convention with its Arcadian shepherds learnedly discoursing on controversial theology is little to us compared with the freshness and the music of the poetry. The irregular cadences, which Spenser invented from his mistaken scanning of Chaucer, reveal musical possibilities in our language not yet exhausted, while the more regular metres of the true tradition show us that inexhaustible power of subtle modulation which carried him victoriously through the long march of the *Faerie Queene*. The charm of this tunefulness of his verse can never fade, and when we read the roundel of Perigot and Willie or Colin's dirge for Dido, we must capitulate to it as fully as that contemporary critic who, in awarding to Spenser the laurel in 1586, named him "the rightest English poet that ever I read."

A. ATTWATER.

CAMBRIDGE,
*December* 1922.

## TO HIS BOOKE

*Goe, little booke! thy selfe present,*
*As child whose parent is unkent,*
*To him that is the president*
*Of Noblesse and of chevalree:*
*And if that Envie barke at thee,*
*As sure it will, for succoure flee*
*Under the shadow of his wing;*
*And asked who thee forth did bring,*
*A shepheards swaine, saye, did thee sing*
*All as his straying flocke he fedde:*
*And, when his honor has thee redde,*
*Crave pardon for my hardyhedde.*
*But, if that any aske thy name,*
*Say, thou wert base-begot with blame;*
*For-thy thereof thou takest shame.*
*And, when thou art past jeopardee,*
*Come tell me what was sayd of mee,*
*And I will send more after thee.*

IMMERITÔ.

# THE SHEPHEARDS CALENDER

## JANUARIE

### ÆGLOGA PRIMA. ARGUMENT

In this fyrst Æglogue Colin Cloute, a shepheardes boy,
complaineth him of his unfortunate love, being but
newly (as semeth) enamoured of a countrie lasse called
Rosalinde: with which strong affection being very sore
traveled, he compareth his carefull case to the sadde
season of the yeare, to the frostie ground, to the frosen
trees, and to his owne winter-beaten flocke. And,
lastlye, fynding himselfe robbed of all former pleasaunce
and delights, hee breaketh his Pipe in peeces, and casteth
him selfe to the ground.

### COLIN CLOUTE

A SHEPEHEARDS boye, (no better doe him call,)
When Winters wastful spight was almost spent,
All in a sunneshine day, as did befall,
Led forth his flock, that had bene long ypent:
  So faynt they woxe, and feeble in the folde,
  That now unnethes their feete could them uphold.

All as the Sheepe, such was the shepeheards looke,
For pale and wanne he was, (alas the while!)
May seeme he lovd, or els some care he tooke;
Well couth he tune his pipe and frame his stile:
  Tho to a hill his faynting flocke he ledde,
  And thus him playnd, the while his shepe there fedde.

'Ye Gods of love, that pitie lovers payne,
(If any gods the paine of lovers pitie,)
Looke from above, where you in joyes remaine,
And bowe your eares unto my dolefull dittie:
  And, Pan, thou shepheards God that once didst love,
  Pitie the paines that thou thy selfe didst prove.

*unnethes*, scarcely.

'Thou barrein ground, whome winters wrath hath
    wasted,
Art made a myrrhour to behold my plight:
Whilome thy fresh spring flowrd, and after hasted
Thy sommer prowde, with Daffadillies dight;
    And now is come thy wynters stormy state,
    Thy mantle mard, wherein thou maskedst late.

'Such rage as winters reigneth in my heart,
My life-bloud friesing with unkindly cold;
Such stormy stoures do breede my balefull smart,
As if my yeare were wast and woxen old;
    And yet, alas! but now my spring begonne,
    And yet, alas! yt is already donne.

'You naked trees, whose shady leaves are lost,
Wherein the byrds were wont to build their bowre,
And now are clothd with mosse and hoary frost,
Instede of bloosmes, wherewith your buds did flowre;
    I see your teares that from your boughes doe raine,
    Whose drops in drery ysicles remaine.

'All so my lustfull leafe is drye and sere,
My timely buds with wayling all are wasted;
The blossome which my braunch of youth did beare
With breathed sighes is blowne away and blasted;
    And from mine eyes the drizling teares descend,
    As on your boughes the ysicles depend.

'Thou feeble flocke, whose fleece is rough and rent,
Whose knees are weake through fast and evill fare,
Mayst witnesse well, by thy ill governement,
Thy maysters mind is overcome with care:
    Thou weake, I wanne; thou leane, I quite forlorne:
    With mourning pyne I; you with pyning mourne.

*stoures*, tumults.

'A thousand sithes I curse that carefull hower
Wherein I longd the neighbour towne to see,
And eke tenne thousand sithes I blesse the stoure
Wherein I sawe so fayre a sight as shee:
   Yet all for naught: such sight hath bred my bane.
   Ah, God! that love should breede both joy and payne!

'It is not Hobbinol wherefore I plaine,
Albee my love he seeke with dayly suit;
His clownish gifts and curtsies I disdaine,
His kiddes, his cracknelles, and his early fruit.
   Ah, foolish Hobbinol! thy gyfts bene vayne;
   Colin them gives to Rosalind againe.

'I love thilke lasse, (alas! why doe I love?)
And am forlorne, (alas! why am I lorne?)
Shee deignes not my good will, but doth reprove,
And of my rurall musicke holdeth scorne.
   Shepheards devise she hateth as the snake,
   And laughes the songs that Colin Clout doth make.

'Wherefore, my pype, albee rude Pan thou please,
Yet for thou pleasest not where most I would:
And thou, unlucky Muse, that wontst to ease
My musing mynd, yet canst not when thou should;
   Both pype and Muse shall sore the while abye.'
   So broke his oaten pype, and downe dyd lye.

By that, the welked Phœbus gan availe
His weary waine; and nowe the frosty Night
Her mantle black through heaven gan overhaile:
Which seene, the pensife boy, halfe in despight,
   Arose, and homeward drove his sonned sheepe,
   Whose hanging heads did seeme his carefull case to
     weepe.

     *sithes*, times.     *availe*, bring down.

## FEBRUARIE

### ÆGLOGA SECUNDA.   ARGUMENT

This Æglogue is rather morall and generall, then bent
to any secrete or particular purpose. It specially con-
teyneth a discourse of old age, in the persone of Thenot,
an olde Shepheard, who for his crookednesse and un-
lustinesse is scorned of Cuddie, an unhappy Heardmans
boye. The matter very well accordeth with the season
of the moneth, the yeare now drouping, and as it were
drawing to his last age. For as in this time of yeare, so
then in our bodies, there is a dry and withering cold,
which congealeth the crudled blood, and frieseth the
wetherbeaten flesh with stormes of Fortune, and hoare
frosts of Care. To which purpose the olde man telleth
a tale of the Oake and the Bryer, so lively, and so
feelingly, as, if the thing were set forth in some Picture
before our eyes, more plainly could not appeare.

### CUDDIE.   THENOT

#### *Cuddie*

Ah for pittie! wil rancke Winters rage
These bitter blasts never ginne tasswage?
The kene cold blowes through my beaten hyde,
All as I were through the body gryde:
My ragged rontes all shiver and shake,
As doen high Towers in an earthquake:
They wont in the wind wagge their wrigle tayles,
Perke as a Peacock; but now it avales.

#### *Thenot*

Lewdly complainest thou, laesie ladde,
Of Winters wracke for making thee sadde.
Must not the world wend in his commun course,
From good to badd, and from badde to worse,
From worse unto that is worst of all,

       *gryde*, pierced.        *rontes*, young bullocks.

And then returne to his former fall?
Who will not suffer the stormy time,
Where will he live tyll the lusty prime?
Selfe have I worne out thrise threttie yeares,
Some in much joy, many in many teares,
Yet never complained of cold nor heate,
Of Sommers flame, nor of Winters threat,
Ne ever was to Fortune foeman,
But gently tooke that ungently came;
And ever my flocke was my chiefe care,
Winter or Sommer they mought well fare.

### Cuddie

No marveile, Thenot, if thou can beare
Cherefully the Winters wrathful cheare;
For Age and Winter accord full nie,
This chill, that cold; this crooked, that wrye;
And as the lowring Wether lookes downe,
So semest thou like Good Fryday to frowne:
But my flowring youth is foe to frost,
My shippe unwont in stormes to be tost.

### Thenot

The soveraigne of seas he blames in vaine,
That, once sea-beate, will to sea againe:
So loytring live you little heardgroomes,
Keeping your beastes in the budded broomes:
And, when the shining sunne laugheth once,
You deemen the Spring is come attonce;
Tho gynne you, fond flyes! the cold to scorne,
And, crowing in pypes made of greene corne,
You thinken to be Lords of the yeare;
But eft, when ye count you freed from feare,
Comes the breme Winter with chamfred browes,

*breme*, cold.          *chamfred*, chapped.

Full of wrinckles and frostie furrowes,
Drerily shooting his stormy darte,
Which cruddles the blood and pricks the harte:
Then is your carelesse corage accoied,
Your carefull heards with cold bene annoied:
Then paye you the price of your surquedrie,
With weeping, and wayling, and misery.

### Cuddie

Ah, foolish old man! I scorne thy skill,
That wouldest me my springing youngth to spil:
I deeme thy braine emperished bee
Through rusty elde, that hath rotted thee:
Or sicker thy head veray tottie is,
So on thy corbe shoulder it leanes amisse.
Now thy selfe hast lost both lopp and topp,
Als my budding braunch thou wouldest cropp;
But were thy yeares greene, as now bene myne,
To other delights they would encline:
Tho wouldest thou learne to caroll of Love,
And hery with hymnes thy lasses glove;
Tho wouldest thou pype of Phyllis prayse;
But Phyllis is myne for many dayes.
I wonne her with a gyrdle of gelt,
Embost with buegle about the belt:
Such an one shepeheards would make full faine;
Such an one would make thee younge againe.

### Thenot

Thou art a fon of thy love to boste;
All that is lent to love wyll be lost.

| | |
|---|---|
| *accoied*, daunted. | *corbe*, crooked. |
| *surquedrie*, pride. | *hery*, worship. |
| *sicker*, surely. | *fon*, fool. |

### Cuddie

Seest howe brag yond Bullocke beares,
So smirke, so smoothe, his pricked eares?
His hornes bene as broade as Rainebowe bent,
His dewelap as lythe as lasse of Kent:
See howe he venteth into the wynd;
Weenest of love is not his mynd?
Seemeth thy flocke thy counsell can,
So lustlesse bene they, so weake, so wan;
Clothed with cold, and hoary wyth frost,
Thy flocks father his corage hath lost.
Thy Ewes, that wont to have blowen bags,
Like wailefull widdowes hangen their crags;
The rather Lambes bene starved with cold,
All for their Maister is lustlesse and old.

### Thenot

Cuddie, I wote thou kenst little good,
So vainely tadvaunce thy headlesse hood;
For youngth is a bubble blown up with breath,
Whose witt is weakenesse, whose wage is death,
Whose way is wildernesse, whose ynne Penaunce,
And stoope-gallaunt Age, the hoste of Greevaunce.
But shall I tel thee a tale of truth,
Which I cond of Tityrus in my youth,
Keeping his sheepe on the hils of Kent?

### Cuddie

To nought more, Thenot, my mind is bent
Then to heare novells of his devise;
They bene so well-thewed, and so wise,
What ever that good old man bespake.

*can*, knows.     *crags*, necks.     *rather*, early.

*Thenot*

Many meete tales of youth did he make,
And some of love, and some of chevalrie;
But none fitter then this to applie.
Now listen a while and hearken the end.
  There grewe an aged Tree on the greene,
A goodly Oake sometime had it bene,
With armes full strong and largely displayd,
But of their leaves they were disarayde:
The bodie bigge, and mightely pight,
Throughly rooted, and of wonderous hight;
Whilome had bene the King of the field,
And mochell mast to the husband did yielde,
And with his nuts larded many swine:
But now the gray mosse marred his rine;
His bared boughes were beaten with stormes,
His toppe was bald, and wasted with wormes,
His honor decayed, his braunches sere.
  Hard by his side grewe a bragging Brere,
Which proudly thrust into Thelement,
And seemed to threat the Firmament:
It was embellisht with blossomes fayre,
And thereto aye wonned to repayre
The shepheards daughters to gather flowres,
To peinct their girlonds with his colowres;
And in his small bushes used to shrowde
The sweete Nightingale singing so lowde;
Which made this foolish Brere wexe so bold,
That on a time he cast him to scold
And snebbe the good Oake, for he was old.
  'Why standst there (quoth he) thou brutish blocke?
Nor for fruict nor for shadowe serves thy stocke;
Seest how fresh my flowers bene spredde,

*pight*, fixed.

Dyed in Lilly white and Cremsin redde,
With Leaves engrained in lusty greene;
Colours meete to clothe a mayden Queene?
Thy wast bignes but combers the grownd,
And dirks the beauty of my blossomes rownd:
The mouldie mosse, which thee accloieth,
My Sinamon smell too much annoieth:
Wherefore soone I rede thee hence remove,
Least thou the price of my displeasure prove.'
So spake this bold brere with great disdaine:
Little him aunswered the Oake againe,
But yeelded, with shame and greefe adawed,
That of a weede he was overcrawed.

Yt chaunced after upon a day,
The Hus-bandman selfe to come that way,
Of custome for to survewe his grownd,
And his trees of state in compasse rownd:
Him when the spitefull brere had espyed,
Causelesse complained, and lowdly cryed
Unto his lord, stirring up sterne strife.

'O, my liege Lord! the God of my life!
Pleaseth you ponder your Suppliants plaint,
Caused of wrong and cruell constraint,
Which I your poore Vassall dayly endure;
And, but your goodnes the same recure,
Am like for desperate doole to dye,
Through felonous force of mine enemie.'

Greatly aghast with this piteous plea,
Him rested the goodman on the lea,
And badde the Brere in his plaint proceede.
With painted words tho gan this proude weede
(As most usen Ambitious folke:)
His colowred crime with craft to cloke.

*adawed*, daunted.

'Ah, my soveraigne! Lord of creatures all,
Thou placer of plants both humble and tall,
Was not I planted of thine owne hand,
To be the primrose of all thy land;
With flowring blossomes to furnish the prime,
And scarlot berries in Sommer time?
How falls it then that this faded Oake,
Whose bodie is sere, whose braunches broke,
Whose naked Armes stretch unto the fyre,
Unto such tyrannie doth aspire;
Hindering with his shade my lovely light,
And robbing me of the swete sonnes sight?
So beate his old boughes my tender-side,
That oft the bloud springeth from woundes wyde;
Untimely my flowres forced to fall,
That bene the honor of your Coronall:
And oft he lets his cancker-wormes light
Upon my braunches, to worke me more spight;
And oft his hoarie locks downe doth cast,
Where-with my fresh flowretts bene defast:
For this, and many more such outrage,
Craving your goodlihead to aswage
The ranckorous rigour of his might,
Nought aske I, but onely to hold my right;
Submitting me to your good sufferance,
And praying to be garded from greevance.'
  To this the Oake cast him to replie
Well as he couth; but his enemie
Had kindled such coles of displeasure,
That the good man noulde stay his leasure,
But home him hasted with furious heate,
Encreasing his wrath with many a threate:
His harmefull Hatchet he hent in hand,

*hent*, caught.

(Alas! that it so ready should stand!)
And to the field alone he speedeth,
(Ay little helpe to harme there needeth!)
Anger nould let him speake to the tree,
Enaunter his rage mought cooled bee;
But to the roote bent his sturdy stroake,
And made many wounds in the wast Oake.
The Axes edge did oft turne againe,
As halfe unwilling to cutte the graine;
Semed, the sencelesse yron dyd feare,
Or to wrong holy eld did forbeare;
For it had bene an auncient tree,
Sacred with many a mysteree,
And often crost with the priestes crewe,
And often halowed with holy-water dewe:
But sike fancies weren foolerie,
And broughten this Oake to this miserye;
For nought mought they quitten him from decay,
For fiercely the good man at him did laye.
The blocke oft groned under the blow,
And sighed to see his neare overthrow.
In fine, the steele had pierced his pitth,
Tho downe to the earth he fell forthwith.
His wonderous weight made the ground to quake,
Thearth shronke under him, and seemed to shake:—
There lyeth the Oake, pitied of none!
  Now stands the Brere like a lord alone,
Puffed up with pryde and vaine pleasaunce;
But all this glee had no continuaunce:
For eftsones Winter gan to approche;
The blustering Boreas did encroche,
And beate upon the solitarie Brere;
For nowe no succoure was seene him nere.
Now gan he repent his pryde to late;

For, naked left and disconsolate,
The byting frost nipt his stalke dead,
The watrie wette weighed downe his head,
And heaped snowe burdned him so sore,
That nowe upright he can stand no more;
And, being downe, is trodde in the durt
Of cattell, and brouzed, and sorely hurt.
Such was thend of this Ambitious brere,
For scorning Eld—

### Cuddie

Now I pray thee, shepheard, tel it not forth:
Here is a long tale, and little worth.
So longe have I listened to thy speche,
That graffed to the ground is my breche:
My hart-blood is wel nigh frorne, I feele,
And my galage growne fast to my heele:
But little ease of thy lewd tale I tasted:
Hye thee home, shepheard, the day is nigh wasted.


# MARCH

#### ÆGLOGA TERTIA.  ARGUMENT

In this Æglogue two shepheards boyes, taking occasion
of the season, beginne to make purpose of love, and
other plesaunce which to spring time is most agreeable.
The speciall meaning hereof is, to give certaine markes
and tokens to know Cupide, the Poets God of Love.
But more particularlye, I thinke, in the person of
Thomalin is meant some secrete freend, who scorned
Love and his knights so long, till at length him selfe
was entangled, and unwares wounded with the dart of
some beautifull regard, which is Cupides arrow.

*galage*, shoe.

## WILLYE.  THOMALIN

*Wil*.  THOMALIN, why sytten we soe,
As weren overwent with woe,
  Upon so fayre a morow?
The joyous time now nighes fast,
That shall alegge this bitter blast,
  And slake the winters sorowe.
*Tho*.  Sicker, Willye, thou warnest well;
For Winters wrath beginnes to quell,
  And pleasant spring appeareth:
The grasse nowe ginnes to be refresht,
The Swallow peepes out of her nest,
  And clowdie Welkin cleareth.
*Wil*.  Seest not thilke same Hawthorne studde,
How bragly it beginnes to budde,
  And utter his tender head?
Flora now calleth forth eche flower,
And bids make readie Maias bowre,
  That newe is upryst from bedde:
Tho shall we sporten in delight,
And learne with Lettice to wexe light,
  That scornefully lookes askaunce;
Tho will we little Love awake,
That nowe sleepeth in Lethe lake,
  And pray him leaden our daunce.
*Tho*.  Willye, I wene thou bee assot;
For lustie Love still sleepeth not,
  But is abroad at his game.
*Wil*.  How kenst thou that he is awoke?
Or hast thy selfe his slomber broke,
  Or made previe to the same?

*Tho.*  No: but happely I hym spyde,
Where in a bush he did him hide,
  With winges of purple and blewe;
And, were not that my sheepe would stray,
The previe marks I would bewray,
  Whereby by chaunce I him knewe.
*Wil.*  Thomalin, have no care for-thy;
My selfe will have a double eye,
  Ylike to my flocke and thine;
For als at home I have a syre,
A stepdame eke, as whott as fyre,
  That dewly adayes counts mine.
*Tho.*  Nay, but thy seeing will not serve,
My sheepe for that may chaunce to swerve,
  And fall into some mischiefe:
For sithens is but the third morowe
That I chaunst to fall asleepe with sorowe
  And waked againe with griefe;
The while thilke same unhappye Ewe,
Whose clouted legge her hurt doth shewe,
  Fell headlong into a dell,
And there unjoynted both her bones:
Mought her necke bene joynted attones,
  She shoulde have neede no more spell;
Thelf was so wanton and so wood,
(But now I trowe can better good,)
  She mought ne gang on the greene.
*Wil.*  Let be, as may be, that is past:
That is to come, let be forecast:
  Now tell us what thou hast seene.
*Tho.*  It was upon a holiday,
When shepheardes groomes han leave to playe,
  I cast to goe a shooting.
Long wandring up and downe the land,

With bowe and bolts in either hand,
  For birds in bushes tooting,
At length within an Yvie todde,
(There shrouded was the little God)
  I heard a busie bustling.
I bent my bolt against the bush,
Listening if any thing did rushe,
  But then heard no more rustling:
Tho, peeping close into the thicke,
Might see the moving of some quicke,
  Whose shape appeared not;
But were it faerie, feend, or snake,
My courage earnd it to awake,
  And manfully thereat shotte.
With that sprong forth a naked swayne
With spotted winges, like Peacocks trayne,
  And laughing lope to a tree;
His gylden quiver at his backe,
And silver bowe, which was but slacke,
  Which lightly he bent at me:
That seeing, I levelde againe
And shott at him with might and maine,
  As thicke as it had hayled.
So long I shott, that al was spent;
Tho pumie stones I hastly hent
  And threwe; but nought availed:
He was so wimble and so wight,
From bough to bough he lepped light,
  And oft the pumies latched.
Therewith affrayd, I ranne away;
But he, that earst seemd but to playe,
  A shaft in earnest snatched,
And hit me running in the heele:

       *todde*, thicket.

For then I little smart did feele,
　But soone it sore encreased;
And now it ranckleth more and more,
And inwardly it festreth sore,
　Ne wote I how to cease it.
*Wil.* Thomalin, I pittie thy plight,
Perdie with Love thou diddest fight:
　I know him by a token;
For once I heard my father say,
How he him caught upon a day,
　(Whereof he wil be wroken)
Entangled in a fowling net,
Which he for carrion Crowes had set
　That in our Peere-tree haunted:
Tho sayd, he was a winged lad,
But bowe and shafts as then none had,
　Els had he sore be daunted.
But see, the Welkin thicks apace,
And stouping Phebus steepes his face:
　Yts time to hast us homeward.

## APRIL

### ÆGLOGA QUARTA. ARGUMENT

This Æglogue is purposely intended to the honor and
prayse of our most gracious sovereigne, Queene Eliza-
beth. The speakers herein be Hobbinoll and Thenott,
two shepheardes: the which Hobbinoll, being before
mentioned greatly to have loved Colin, is here set forth
more largely, complayning him of that boyes great
misadventure in Love; whereby his mynd was alienate
and withdrawen not onely from him, who moste loved
him, but also from all former delightes and studies, as
well in pleasaunt pyping, as conning ryming and singing,
and other his laudable exercises. Whereby he taketh

occasion, for proofe of his more excellencie and skill
in poetrie, to recorde a songe, which the sayd Colin
sometime made in honor of her Majestie, whom
abruptely he termeth Elysa.

### THENOT.  HOBBINOLL

*The.*  TELL me, good Hobbinoll, what garres thee
    greete?
  What? hath some Wolfe thy tender Lambes ytorne?
Or is thy Bagpype broke, that soundes so sweete?
  Or art thou of thy loved lasse forlorne?

Or bene thine eyes attempred to the yeare,
  Quenching the gasping furrowes thirst with rayne?
Like April shoure so stremes the trickling teares
  Adowne thy cheeke, to quenche thy thristye payne.

*Hob.*  Nor thys, nor that, so muche doeth make me
    mourne,
  But for the ladde, whome long I lovd so deare,
Nowe loves a lasse that all his love doth scorne:
  He, plongd in payne, his tressed locks dooth
    teare.

Shepheards delights he dooth them all forsweare;
  Hys pleasaunt Pipe, whych made us meriment,
He wylfully hath broke, and doth forbeare
  His wonted songs, wherein he all outwent.

*The.*  What is he for a Ladde you so lament?
  Ys love such pinching payne to them that prove?
And hath he skill to make so excellent,
  Yet hath so little skill to brydle love?

      *garres thee greete*, makes thee cry.

A.S.                                                   2

*Hob*. Colin thou kenst, the Southerne shepheardes
    boye;
  Him Love hath wounded with a deadly darte:
Whilome on him was all my care and joye,
    Forcing with gyfts to winne his wanton heart.

But now from me hys madding mynd is starte,
    And woes the Widdowes daughter of the glenne;
So nowe fayre Rosalind hath bredde hys smart,
    So now his frend is chaunged for a frenne.

*The*. But if hys ditties bene so trimly dight,
    I pray thee, Hobbinoll, recorde some one,
The whiles our flockes do graze about in sight,
    And we close shrowded in thys shade alone.

*Hob*. Contented I: then, will I singe his laye
    Of fayre Elisa, Queene of shepheardes all,
Which once he made as by a spring he laye,
    And tuned it unto the Waters fall.

'Ye dayntye Nymphs, that in this blessed brooke
    Doe bathe your brest,
Forsake your watry bowres, and hether looke,
    At my request:
And eke you Virgins, that on Parnasse dwell,
Whence floweth Helicon, the learned well,
    Helpe me to blaze
    Her worthy praise,
Which in her sexe doth all excell.

'Of fayre Elisa be your silver song,
    That blessed wight,
The flowre of Virgins: may shee florish long
    In princely plight!

          *frenne*, stranger.

For shee is Syrinx daughter without spotte,
Which Pan, the shepheards God, of her begot:
   So sprong her grace
   Of heavenly race,
No mortall blemishe may her blotte.

'See, where she sits upon the grassie greene,
   (O seemely sight!)
Yclad in Scarlot, like a mayden Queene,
   And ermines white:
Upon her head a Cremosin coronet,
With Damaske roses and Daffadillies set:
   Bay leaves betweene,
   And primroses greene,
Embellish the sweete Violet.

'Tell me, have ye seene her angelick face,
   Like Phœbe fayre?
Her heavenly haveour, her princely grace,
   Can you well compare?
The Redde rose medled with the White yfere,
In either cheeke depeincten lively chere:
   Her modest eye,
   Her Majestie,
Where have you seene the like but there?

'I sawe Phœbus thrust out his golden hedde,
   Upon her to gaze:
But, when he sawe how broade her beames did spredde,
   It did him amaze.
He blusht to see another Sunne belowe,
Ne durst againe his fyrye face out showe:
   Let him, if he dare,
   His brightnesse compare
With hers, to have the overthrowe.

*yfere*, together.

'Shewe thyselfe, Cynthia, with thy silver rayes,
    And be not abasht:
When shee the beames of her beauty displayes,
    O, how art thou dasht!
But I will not match her with Latonaes seede,
Such follie great sorow to Niobe did breede:
    Now she is a stone,
    And makes dayly mone,
Warning all other to take heede.

'Pan may be proud that ever he begot
    Such a Bellibone;
And Syrinx rejoyse that ever was her lot
    To beare such an one.
Soone as my younglings cryen for the dam
To her will I offer a milkwhite Lamb:
    Shee is my goddesse plaine,
    And I her shepherds swayne,
Albee forswonck and forswatt I am.

'I see Calliope speede her to the place,
    Where my Goddesse shines;
And after her the other Muses trace,
    With their Violines.
Bene they not Bay braunches which they do beare,
All for Elisa in her hand to weare?
    So sweetely they play,
    And sing all the way,
That it a heaven is to heare.

'Lo! how finely the Graces can it foote
    To the Instrument:
They dauncen deffly, and singen soote,
    In their meriment.

*Bellibone*, belle et bonne.

Wants not a fourth Grace, to make the daunce even?
Let that rowme to my Lady be yeven:
   She shal be a Grace,
   To fyll the fourth place,
And reigne with the rest in heaven.

'And whither rennes this bevie of Ladies bright,
   Raunged in a rowe?
They bene all Ladyes of the lake behight,
   That unto her goe.
Chloris, that is the chiefest Nymph of all,
Of Olive braunches beares a Coronall:
   Olives bene for peace,
   When wars doe surcease:
Such for a Princesse bene principall.

'Ye shepheards daughters, that dwell on the greene,
   Hye you there apace:
Let none come there but that Virgins bene,
   To adorne her grace:
And, when you come whereas shee is in place,
See that your rudenesse doe not you disgrace:
   Binde your fillets faste,
   And gird in your waste,
For more finenesse, with a tawdrie lace.

'Bring hether the Pincke and purple Cullambine,
   With Gelliflowres;
Bring Coronations, and Sops in wine,
   Worne of Paramoures:
Strowe me the ground with Daffadowndillies,
And Cowslips, and Kingcups, and loved Lillies:
   The pretie Pawnce,
   And the Chevisaunce,
Shall match with the fayre flowre Delice.

   *Pawnce*, pansy.     *Chevisaunce*, probably wallflower.

'Now ryse up, Elisa, decked as thou art
   In royall aray;
And now ye daintie Damsells may depart
   Eche one her way.
I feare I have troubled your troupes to longe:
Let dame Elisa thanke you for her song:
   And if you come hether
   When Damsines I gether,
I will part them all you among.'

*The*. And was thilk same song of Colins owne making?
   Ah, foolish Boy! that is with love yblent:
Great pittie is, he be in such taking,
   For naught caren that bene so lewdly bent.

*Hob*. Sicker I hold him for a greater fon,
   That loves the thing he cannot purchase.
But let us homeward, for night draweth on,
   And twincling starres the daylight hence chase.

# MAYE

### ÆGLOGA QUINTA. ARGUMENT

In this fifte Æglogue, under the persons of two shepheards, Piers and Palinodie, be represented two formes
of pastoures or Ministers, or the Protestant and the
Catholique: whose chiefe talke standeth in reasoning,
whether the life of the one must be like the other: with
whom having shewed, that it is daungerous to mainteine
any felowship, or give too much credit to their colour-
able and feyned good will, he telleth him a tale of the
foxe, that, by such a counterpoynt of craftines, deceived
and devoured the credulous kidde.

### PALINODE.  PIERS

*Palinode.*  Is not thilke the mery moneth of May,
When love-lads masken in fresh aray?
How falles it, then, we no merrier bene,
Ylike as others, girt in gawdy greene?
Our bloncket liveryes bene all to sadde
For thilke same season, when all is ycladd
With pleasaunce: the grownd with grasse, the Woods
With greene leaves, the bushes with bloosming buds.
Yougthes folke now flocken in every where,
To gather May bus-kets and smelling brere:
And home they hasten the postes to dight,
And all the Kirke pillours eare day light,
With Hawthorne buds, and swete Eglantine,
And girlonds of roses, and Sopps in wine.
Such merimake holy Saints doth queme,
But we here sitten as drownd in a dreme.
    *Piers.*  For Younkers, Palinode, such follies fitte,
But we tway bene men of elder witt.
    *Pal.*  Sicker this morrowe, no lenger agoe,
I sawe a shole of shepeheardes outgoe
With singing, and shouting, and jolly chere:
Before them yode a lusty Tabrere,
That to the many a Horne-pype playd,
Whereto they dauncen, eche one with his mayd.
To see those folkes make such jovysaunce,
Made my heart after the pype to daunce:
Tho to the greene Wood they speeden hem all,
To fetchen home May with their musicall:
And home they bringen in a royall throne,
Crowned as king: and his Queene attone

*bus-kets*, little bushes.    *queme*, please.    *yode*, went.

Was Lady Flora, on whom did attend
A fayre flocke of Faeries, and a fresh bend
Of lovely Nymphs. (O that I were there,
To helpen the Ladyes their Maybush beare!)
Ah! Piers, bene not thy teeth on edge, to thinke
How great sport they gaynen with little swinck?
   *Piers.* Perdie, so farre am I from envie,
That their fondnesse inly I pitie:
Those faytours little regarden their charge,
While they, letting their sheepe runne at large,
Passen their time, that should be sparely spent,
In lustihede and wanton meryment.
Thilke same bene shepeheardes for the Devils stedde,
That playen while their flockes be unfedde:
Well is it seene theyr sheepe bene not their owne,
That letten them runne at randon alone:
But they bene hyred for little pay
Of other, that caren as little as they
What fallen the flocke, so they han the fleece,
And get all the gayne, paying but a peece.
I muse, what account both these will make;
The one for the hire which he doth take,
And thother for leaving his Lords taske,
When great Pan account of shepeherdes shall aske.
   *Pal.* Sicker, now I see thou speakest of spight,
All for thou lackest somedele their delight.
I (as I am) had rather be envied,
All were it of my foe, then fonly pitied:
And yet, if neede were, pitied would be,
Rather then other should scorne at me:
For pittied is mishappe that nas remedie,
But scorned bene dedes of fond foolerie.
What shoulden shepheards other things tend,

*faytours*, vagabonds.

Then, sith their God his good does them send,
Reapen the fruite thereof, that is pleasure,
The while they here liven at ease and leasure?
For, when they bene dead, their good is ygoe,
They sleepen in rest, well as other moe:
Tho with them wends what they spent in cost,
But what they left behind them is lost.
Good is no good, but if it be spend;
God giveth good for none other end.
   *Piers.*  Ah! Palinodie, thou art a worldes childe:
Who touches Pitch, mought needes be defilde;
But shepheards (as Algrind used to say)
Mought not live ylike as men of the laye.
With them it sits to care for their heire,
Enaunter their heritage doe impaire.
They must provide for meanes of maintenaunce,
And to continue their wont countenaunce:
But shepheard must walke another way,
Sike worldly sovenance he must forsay.
The sonne of his loines why should he regard
To leave enriched with that he hath spard?
Should not thilke God, that gave him that good,
Eke cherish his child, if in his wayes he stood?
For if he mislive in leudnes and lust,
Little bootes all the welth and the trust,
That his father left by inheritaunce;
All will be soone wasted with misgovernaunce;
But through this, and other their miscreaunce
They maken many a wrong chevisaunce,
Heaping up waves of welth and woe,
The floddes whereof shall them overflowe.
Sike mens follie I cannot compare
Better then to the Apes folish care,

     *sovenance*, memory.     *chevisaunce*, enterprise.

That is so enamoured of her young one,
(And yet, God wote, such cause hath she none)
That with her hard hold, and straight embracing,
She stoppeth the breath of her youngling.
So often times, when as good is meant,
Evil ensueth of wrong entent.
　　The time was once, and may againe retorne,
(For ought may happen, that hath bene beforne)
When shepeheards had none inheritaunce,
Ne of land, nor fee in sufferaunce,
But what might arise of the bare sheepe,
(Were it more or lesse) which they did keepe.
Well ywis was it with shepheards thoe:
Nought having, nought feared they to forgoe;
For Pan himselfe was their inheritaunce,
And little them served for their mayntenaunce.
The shepheards God so wel them guided,
That of nought they were unprovided;
Butter enough, honye, milke, and whay,
And their flockes fleeces them to araye:
But tract of time, and long prosperitie,
That nource of vice, this of insolencie,
Lulled the shepheards in such securitie,
That, not content with loyall obeysaunce,
Some gan to gape for greedie governaunce,
And match them selfe with mighty potentates,
Lovers of Lordship, and troublers of states.
Tho gan shepheards swaines to looke aloft,
And leave to live hard, and learne to ligge soft:
Tho, under colour of shepeheards, somewhile
There crept in Wolves, ful of fraude, and guile,
That often devoured their owne sheepe,
And often the shepheards that did hem keepe:
This was the first sourse of shepheards sorowe,

That now nill be quitt with baile nor borrowe.
  *Pal.*  Three thinges to beare bene very burdenous,
But the fourth to forbeare is outragious:
Wemen, that of Loves longing once lust,
Hardly forbearen, but have it they must:
So when choler is inflamed with rage,
Wanting revenge, is hard to asswage:
And who can counsell a thristie soule,
With patience to forbeare the offred bowle?
But of all burdens, that a man can beare,
Most is, a fooles talke to beare and to heare.
I wene the Geaunt has not such a weight,
That beares on his shoulders the heavens height.
Thou findest faulte where nys to be found,
And buildest strong warke upon a weake ground:
Thou raylest on, right withouten reason,
And blamest hem much for small encheason.
How shoulden shepheardes live, if not so?
What! should they pynen in payne and woe?
Nay, say I thereto, by my deare borrowe,
If I may rest, I nill live in sorrowe.
  Sorrowe ne neede be hastened on,
For he will come, without calling, anone.
While times enduren of tranquillitie,
Usen we freely our felicitie;
For, when approchen the stormie stowres,
We mought with our shoulders beare of the sharpe
       showres;
And, sooth to sayne, nought seemeth sike strife,
That shepheardes so witen ech others life,
And layen her faults the world beforne,
The while their foes done eache of hem scorne.
Let none mislike of that may not be mended:

      *encheason*, occasion.     *witen*, blame.

So conteck soone by concord mought be ended.

*Piers.* Shepheard, I list none accordaunce make
With shepheard that does the right way forsake:
And of the twaine, if choice were to me,
Had lever my foe then my freend he be;
For what concord han light and darke sam?
Or what peace has the Lion with the Lambe?
Such faitors, when their false harts bene hidde,
Will doe as did the Foxe by the Kidde.

*Pal.* Now, Piers, of felowship, tell us that saying:
For the Ladde can keepe both our flockes from
      straying.

*Piers.* Thilke same Kidde (as I can well devise)
Was too very foolish and unwise;
For on a tyme, in Sommer season,
The Gate her dame, that had good reason,
Yode forth abroade unto the greene wood,
To brouze, or play, or what shee thought good:
But, for she had a motherly care
Of her young sonne, and wit to beware,
Shee set her youngling before her knee,
That was both fresh and lovely to see,
And full of favour as kidde mought be.
His Vellet head began to shoote out,
And his wreathed hornes gan newly sprout:
The blossomes of lust to bud did beginne,
And spring forth ranckly under his chinne.
'My Sonne,' (quoth she and with that gan weepe,
For carefull thoughts in her heart did creepe)
'God blesse thee, poore Orphane! as he mought me,
And send thee joy of thy jollitee.
Thy father,' (that word she spake with payne,
For a sigh had nigh rent her heart in twaine)

      *conteck*, strife.     *sam*, together.

'Thy father, had he lived this day,
To see the braunche of his body displaie,
How would he have joyed at this sweete sight!
But ah! false Fortune such joy did him spight,
And cutte of hys dayes with untimely woe,
Betraying him into the traines of hys foe.
Now I, a waylfull widdowe behight,
Of my old age have this one delight,
To see thee succeede in thy fathers steade,
And florish in flowres of lusty-head:
For even so thy father his head upheld,
And so his hauty hornes did he weld.'
  Tho marking him with melting eyes,
A thrilling throbbe from her hart did aryse,
And interrupted all her other speache
With some old sorowe that made a newe breache:
Seemed shee sawe in the younglings face
The old lineaments of his fathers grace.
At last her solein silence she broke,
And gan his newe-budded beard to stroke.
'Kiddie, (quoth shee) thou kenst the great care
I have of thy health and thy welfare,
Which many wyld beastes liggen in waite
For to entrap in thy tender state:
But most the Foxe, maister of collusion:
For he has voued thy last confusion.
For-thy, my Kiddie, be ruld by mee,
And never give trust to his trecheree:
And, if he chaunce come when I am abroade,
Sperre the yate fast for feare of fraude:
Ne for all his worst, nor for his best,
Open the dore at his request.'
  So schooled the Gate her wanton sonne,

*Sperre*, shut.

That answerd his mother, all should be done.
Tho went the pensife Damme out of dore,
And chaunst to stomble at the threshold flore:
Her stombling steppe some what her amazed,
(For such, as signes of ill luck, bene dispraised;)
Yet forth shee yode, thereat halfe aghast:
And Kiddie the dore sperred after her fast.
It was not long, after shee was gone,
But the false Foxe came to the dore anone:
Not as a Foxe, for then he had be kend,
But all as a poore pedler he did wend,
Bearing a trusse of tryfles at hys backe,
As bells, and babes, and glasses, in hys packe:
A Biggen he had got about his brayne,
For in his headpeace he felt a sore payne:
His hinder heele was wrapt in a clout,
For with great cold he had gotte the gout.
There at the dore he cast me downe hys pack,
And layd him downe, and groned, 'Alack! Alack!
Ah, deare Lord! and sweete Saint Charitee!
That some good body woulde once pitie mee!'
  Well heard Kiddie al this sore constraint,
And lengd to know the cause of his complaint:
Tho, creeping close behind the Wickets clink,
Prevelie he peeped out through a chinck,
Yet not so previlie but the Foxe him spyed;
For deceitfull meaning is double eyed.
  'Ah, good young maister!' (then gan he crye)
'Jesus blesse that sweete face I espye,
And keepe your corpse from the carefull stounds
That in my carrion carcas abounds.'
  The Kidd, pittying hys heavinesse,
Asked the cause of his great distresse,

*Biggen*, cap.        *stounds*, fits.

And also who, and whence that he were?
  Tho he, that had well ycond his lere,
Thus medled his talke with many a teare:
'Sicke, sicke, alas! and little lack of dead,
But I be relieved by your beastlyhead.
I am a poore sheepe, albe my coloure donne,
For with long traveile I am brent in the sonne:
And, if that my Grandsire me sayd be true,
Sicker, I am very sybbe to you:
So be your goodlihead doe not disdayne
The base kinred of so simple swaine.
Of mercye and favour, then, I you pray
With your ayd to fore-stall my neere decay.'
  Tho out of his packe a glasse he tooke,
Wherein while Kiddie unwares did looke,
He was so enamored with the newell,
That nought he deemed deare for the jewell:
Tho opened he the dore, and in came
The false Foxe, as he were starke lame:
His tayle he clapt betwixt his legs twayne,
Lest he should be descried by his trayne.
  Being within, the Kidde made him good glee,
All for the love of the glasse he did see.
After his chere the Pedler can chat,
And tell many lesinges of this and that,
And how he could shewe many a fine knack:
Tho shewed his ware and opened his packe,
All save a bell, which he left behind
In the basket for the Kidde to fynd:
Which when the Kidde stooped downe to catch,
He popt him in, and his basket did latch:
Ne stayed he once the dore to make fast,
But ranne away with him in all hast.

       *sybbe*, kin.     *newell*, new thing.

Home when the doubtfull Damme had her hyde,
She mought see the dore stand open wyde.
All agast, lowdly she gan to call
Her Kidde; but he nould answere at all:
Tho on the flore she saw the merchaundise
Of which her sonne had sette to deere a prise.
What helpe? her Kidde shee knewe well was gone:
Shee weeped and wayled, and made great mone.
Such end had the Kidde, for he nould warned be
Of craft, coloured with simplicitie:
And such end, perdie, does all hem remayne,
That of such falsers freendship bene fayne.

*Pal.* Truly, Piers, thou art beside thy wit,
Furthest fro the marke, weening it to hit.
Now, I pray thee, lette me thy tale borrowe
For our Sir John, to say to morrowe
At the Kerke, when it is holliday;
For well he meanes, but little can say.
But, and if foxes bene so crafty as so,
Much needeth all shepheards hem to knowe.

*Piers.* Of their falshode more could I recount,
But now the bright Sunne gynneth to dismount;
And, for the deawie night now doth nye,
I hold it best for us home to hye.

# JUNE

### ÆGLOGA SEXTA.   ARGUMENT

This Æglogue is wholly vowed to the complayning of
Colins ill successe in his love. For being (as is aforesaid)
enamoured of a country lasse, Rosalind, and having (as
seemeth) founde place in her heart, he lamenteth to his
deare frend Hobbinoll, that he is nowe forsaken un-

faithfully, and in his steede Menalcas, another shepheard, received disloyally. And this is the whole
Argument of this Æglogue.

### Hobbinol. Colin Clout

*Hob.*  Lo! Collin, here the place whose plesaunt syte
From other shades hath weand my wandring mynde:
Tell me, what wants me here to worke delyte?
The simple ayre, the gentle warbling wynde,
So calme, so coole, as no where else I fynde:
The grassye ground with daintye Daysies dight,
The Bramble bush, where Byrds of every kynde
To the waters fall their tunes attemper right.

*Col.*  O happy Hobbinoll! I blesse thy state,
That Paradise hast founde whych Adam lost:
Here wander may thy flocke, early or late,
Withouten dreade of Wolves to bene ytost:
Thy lovely layes here mayst thou freely boste.
But I, unhappy man! whom cruell fate
And angry Gods pursue from coste to coste,
Can nowhere fynd to shroude my lucklesse pate.

*Hob.*  Then, if by me thou list advised be,
Forsake the soyle that so doth thee bewitch:
Leave me those hilles where harbrough nis to see,
Nor holy-bush, nor brere, nor winding witche:
And to the dales resort, where shepheards ritch,
And fruictfull flocks, bene every where to see:
Here no night-ravenes lodge, more black then pitche,
Nor elvish ghosts, nor gastly owles doe flee.

But frendly Faeries, met with many Graces,
And lightfoote Nymphes, can chace the lingring Night
With Heydeguyes, and trimly trodden traces,

*witche*, reed.        *Heydeguyes*, country dance.

Whilst systers nyne, which dwell on Parnasse hight,
Doe make them musick for their more delight:
And Pan himselfe, to kisse their christall faces,
Will pype and daunce when Phœbe shineth bright:
Such pierlesse pleasures have we in these places.

    *Col.* And I, whylst youth and course of carelesse
        yeeres,
Did let me walke withouten lincks of love,
In such delights did joy amongst my peeres:
But ryper age such pleasures doth reprove:
My fancye eke from former follies move
To stayed steps; for time in passing weares,
(As garments doen, which wexen old above,)
And draweth newe delightes with hoary heares.

Tho couth I sing of love, and tune my pype
Unto my plaintive pleas in verses made:
Tho would I seeke for Queene-apples unrype,
To give my Rosalind; and in Sommer shade
Dight gaudy Girlonds was my common trade,
To crowne her golden locks: but yeeres more rype,
And losse of her, whose love as lyfe I wayd,
Those weary wanton toyes away dyd wype.

    *Hob.* Colin, to heare thy rymes and roundelayes,
Which thou wert wont on wastfull hylls to singe,
I more delight then larke in Sommer dayes:
Whose Echo made the neyghbour groves to ring,
And taught the byrds, which in the lower spring
Did shroude in shady leaves from sonny rayes,
Frame to thy songe their chereful cheriping,
Or hold theyr peace, for shame of thy swete layes.

I sawe Calliope wyth Muses moe,
Soone as thy oaten pype began to sound.

Theyr yvory Luyts and Tamburins forgoe,
And from the fountaine, where they sat around,
Renne after hastely thy silver sound;
But, when they came where thou thy skill didst showe,
They drewe abacke, as halfe with shame confound
Shepheard to see them in theyr art outgoe.

 *Col.* Of Muses, Hobbinol, I conne no skill,
For they bene daughters of the hyghest Jove,
And holden scorne of homely shepheards quill:
For sith I heard that Pan with Phœbus strove,
Which him to much rebuke and Daunger drove,
I never lyst presume to Parnasse hyll,
But, pyping lowe in shade of lowly grove,
I play to please myselfe, all be it ill.

Nought weigh I who my song doth prayse or blame,
Ne strive to winne renowne, or passe the rest:
With shepheard sittes not followe flying fame,
But feede his flocke in fields where falls hem best.
I wote my rymes bene rough, and rudely drest;
The fytter they my carefull case to frame:
Enough is me to paint out my unrest,
And poore my piteous plaints out in the same.

The God of shepheards, Tityrus, is dead,
Who taught me homely, as I can, to make;
He, whilst he lived, was the soveraigne head
Of shepheards all that bene with love ytake:
Well couth he wayle his Woes, and lightly slake
The flames which love within his heart had bredd,
And tell us mery tales to keepe us wake,
The while our sheepe about us safely fedde.

Nowe dead he is, and lyeth wrapt in lead,
(O! why should Death on hym such outrage showe?)

And all hys passing skil with him is fledde,
The fame whereof doth dayly greater growe.
But, if on me some little drops would flowe
Of that the spring was in his learned hedde,
I soone would learne these woods to wayle my woe,
And teache the trees their trickling teares to shedde.

Then should my plaints, causd of discurtesee,
As messengers of this my painfull plight,
Flye to my love, where ever that she bee,
And pierce her heart with poynt of worthy wight,
As shee deserves that wrought so deadly spight.
And thou, Menalcas, that by trecheree
Didst underfong my lasse to wexe so light,
Shouldest well be knowne for such thy villanee.

But since I am not as I wish I were,
Ye gentle Shepheards, which your flocks do feede,
Whether on hylls, or dales, or other where,
Beare witnesse all of thys so wicked deede:
And tell the lasse, whose flowre is woxe a weede,
And faultlesse fayth is turned to faithlesse fere,
That she the truest shepheards hart made bleede,
That lyves on earth, and loved her most dere.

*Hob.* O, carefull Colin! I lament thy case;
Thy teares would make the hardest flint to flowe!
Ah, faithlesse Rosalind and voide of grace,
That art the roote of all this ruthfull woe!
But now is time, I gesse, homeward to goe:
Then ryse, ye blessed Flocks, and home apace,
Least night with stealing steppes doe you forsloe,
And wett your tender Lambes that by you trace.

*wight*, blame.    *underfong*, undermine.    *forsloe*, delay.

## JULYE

ÆGLOGA SEPTIMA.   ARGUMENT

This Æglogue is made in the honour and commendation
of good shepeheardes, and to the shame and disprayse
of proude and ambitious Pastours: Such as Morrell is
here imagined to bee.

### THOMALIN. MORRELL

*Tho.*  Is not thilke same a goteheard prowde,
    That sittes on yonder bancke,
Whose straying heard them selfe doth shrowde
    Emong the bushes rancke?
*Mor.*  What, ho! thou jollye shepheards swayne,
    Come up the hyll to me;
Better is then the lowly playne,
    Als for thy flocke and thee.
*Thom.*  Ah! God shield, man, that I should clime,
    And learne to looke alofte;
This reede is ryfe, that oftentime
    Great clymbers fall unsoft.
In humble dales is footing fast,
    The trode is not so tickle:
And though one fall through heedlesse hast,
    Yet is his misse not mickle.
And now the Sonne hath reared up
    His fyerie-footed teme,
Making his way betweene the Cuppe
    And golden Diademe:
The rampant Lyon hunts he fast,
    With dogges of noysome breath,
Whose balefull barking bringes in hast
    Pyne, plagues, and dreery death.

Agaynst his cruell scortching heate,
  Where hast thou coverture?
The wastefull hylls unto his threate
  Is a playne overture.
But, if thee lust to holden chat
  With seely shepherds swayne,
Come downe, and learne the little what,
  That Thomalin can sayne.
*Mor.*  Syker, thous but a laesie loord,
  And rekes much of thy swinck,
That with fond termes, and witlesse words,
  To blere mine eyes doest thinke.
In evill houre thou hentest in hond
  Thus holy hylles to blame,
For sacred unto saints they stond,
  And of them han theyr name.
St. Michels Mount who does not know,
  That wardes the Westerne coste?
And of St. Brigets bowre, I trow,
  All Kent can rightly boaste:
And they that con of Muses skill
  Sayne most-what, that they dwell
(As goteheards wont) upon a hill,
  Beside a learned well.
And wonned not the great God Pan
  Upon mount Olivet,
Feeding the blessed flocke of Dan,
  Which dyd himselfe beget?
*Thom.*  O blessed sheepe! O shepheard great!
  That bought his flocke so deare,
And them did save with bloudy sweat
  From Wolves that would them teare.
*Mor.*  Besyde, as holy fathers sayne,
  There is a hyllye place,

Where Titan ryseth from the mayne
   To renne hys dayly race,
Upon whose toppe the starres bene stayed,
   And all the skie doth leane;
There is the cave where Phœbe layed
   The shepheard long to dreame.
Whilome there used shepheards all
   To feede theyr flocks at will,
Till by his foly one did fall,
   That all the rest did spill.
And, sithens shepheardes bene forsayd
   From places of delight,
For-thy I weene thou be affrayd
   To clime this hilles height.
Of Synah can I tell thee more,
   And of our Ladyes bowre;
But little needes to strow my store,
   Suffice this hill of our.
Here han the holy Faunes recourse,
   And Sylvanes haunten rathe;
Here has the salt Medway his sourse,
   Wherein the Nymphes doe bathe;
The salt Medway, that trickling stremis
   Adowne the dales of Kent,
Till with his elder brother Themis
   His brackish waves be meynt.
Here growes Melampode every where,
   And Teribinth, good for Gotes:
The one my madding kiddes to smere,
   The next to heale theyr throtes.
Hereto, the hills bene nigher heven,
   And thence the passage ethe;

    *meynt*, mingled.     *ethe*, easy.

As well can prove the piercing levin,
    That seeldome falles bynethe.
*Thom.* Syker, thou speakes lyke a lewde lorrell,
    Of Heaven to demen so;
How be I am but rude and borrell,
    Yet nearer wayes I knowe.
To Kerke the narre, from God more farre,
    Has bene an old-sayd sawe,
And he, that strives to touch a starre,
    Oft stombles at a strawe.
Alsoone may shepheard clymbe to skye
    That leades in lowly dales,
As Goteherd prowd, that, sitting hye,
    Upon the Mountaine sayles.
My seely sheepe like well belowe,
    They neede not Melampode:
For they bene hale enough, I trowe,
    And liken theyr abode;
But, if they with thy Gotes should yede,
    They soone myght be corrupted,
Or like not of the frowie fede,
    Or with the weedes be glutted.
The hylls where dwelled holy saints
    I reverence and adore:
Not for themselfe, but for the sayncts
    Which han be dead of yore.
And nowe they bene to heaven forewent,
    Theyr good is with them goe:
Theyr sample onely to us lent,
    That als we mought doe soe.
Shepheards they weren of the best,
    And lived in lowlye leas:
And, sith theyr soules bene now at rest,

*lorrell*, an idle fellow.    *borrell*, a rustic.    *frowie*, musty.

Why done we them disease?
Such one he was (as I have heard
    Old Algrind often sayne)
That whilome was the first shepheard,
    And lived with little gayne:
And meeke he was, as meeke mought be,
    Simple as simple sheepe;
Humble, and like in eche degree
    The flocke which he did keepe.
Often he used of hys keepe
    A sacrifice to bring,
Nowe with a Kidde, now with a sheepe,
    The Altars hallowing.
So lowted he unto hys Lord,
    Such favour couth he fynd,
That sithens never was abhord
    The simple shepheards kynd.
And such, I weene, the brethren were
    That came from Canaän:
The brethren twelve, that kept yfere
    The flockes of mighty Pan.
But nothing such thilk shephearde was
    Whom Ida hyll dyd beare,
That left hys flocke to fetch a lasse,
    Whose love he bought to deare;
For he was proude, that ill was payd,
    (No such mought shepheards bee)
And with lewde lust was overlayd:
    Tway things doen ill agree.
But shepheard mought be meeke and mylde,
    Well-eyed, as Argus was,
With fleshly follyes undefyled,
    And stoute as steede of brasse.

*lowted*, did reverence.

Sike one (sayd Algrind) Moses was,
    That sawe hys makers face,
His face, more cleare then Christall glasse,
    And spake to him in place.
This had a brother (his name I knewe)
    The first of all his cote,
A shepheard trewe, yet not so true
    As he that earst I hote.
Whilome all these were lowe and lief,
    And loved their flocks to feede;
They never stroven to be chiefe,
    And simple was theyr weede:
But now (thanked be God therefore)
    The world is well amend,
Their weedes bene not so nighly wore;
    Such simplesse mought them shend:
They bene yclad in purple and pall,
    So hath theyr god them blist;
They reigne and rulen over all,
    And lord it as they list:
Ygyrt with belts of glitterand gold,
    (Mought they good sheepeheards bene?)
Theyr Pan theyr sheepe to them has sold,
    I saye as some have seene.
For Palinode (if thou him ken)
    Yode late on Pilgrimage
To Rome, (if such be Rome) and then
    He saw thilke misusage;
For shepeheards (sayd he) there doen leade,
    As Lordes done other where;
Theyr sheepe han crustes, and they the bread;
    The chippes, and they the chere:
They han the fleece, and eke the flesh,

*shend*, disgrace.

(O, seely sheepe, the while!)
The corne is theyrs, let other thresh,
   Their handes they may not file.
They han great stores and thriftye stockes,
   Great freendes and feeble foes:
What neede hem caren for their flocks,
   Theyr boyes can looke to those.
These wisards welter in welths waves,
   Pampred in pleasures deepe:
They han fatte kernes, and leany knaves,
   Their fasting flockes to keepe.
Sike mister men bene all misgone,
   They heapen hylles of wrath;
Sike syrlye shepheards han we none,
   They keepen all the path.
*Mor.* Here is a great deale of good matter
   Lost for lacke of telling:
Now, sicker, I see thou doest but clatter,
   Harme may come of melling.
Thou medlest more then shall have thanke,
   To wyten shepheards welth:
When folke bene fat, and riches rancke,
   It is a signe of helth.
But say me, what is Algrind, he
   That is so oft bynempt?
*Thom.* He is a shepheard great in gree,
   But hath bene long ypent.
One daye he sat upon a hyll,
   (As now thou wouldest me:
But I am taught, by Algrinds ill,
   To love the lowe degree);
For sitting so with bared scalpe,
   An Eagle sored hye,

*mister*, **manner.**       *bynempt*, **named.**

That, weening hys whyte head was chalke,
    A shell-fish downe let flye:
She weend the shell-fishe to have broke,
    But therewith bruzd his brayne;
So now, astonied with the stroke,
    He lyes in lingring payne.
*Mor.* Ah! good Algrind! his hap was ill,
    But shall be better in time.
Now farwell, shepheard, sith thys hyll
    Thou hast such doubt to climbe.


## AUGUST

### ÆGLOGA OCTAVA. ARGUMENT

In this Æglogue is set forth a delectable controversie,
made in imitation of that in Theocritus: whereto also
Virgile fashioned his third and seventh Æglogue. They
choose for umpere of their strife, Cuddie, a neatheards
boye; who, having ended their cause, reciteth also
himselfe a proper song, whereof Colin, he sayth, was
Authour.

### WILLIE. PERIGOT. CUDDIE

*Wil.* TELL me, Perigot, what shalbe the game,
    Wherefore with myne thou dare thy musick matche?
Or bene thy Bagpypes renne farre out of frame?
    Or hath the Crampe thy joynts benomd with ache?
*Per.* Ah! Willye, when the hart is ill assayde,
How can Bagpipe or joynts be well apayd?

*Wil.* What the foule evill hath thee so bestadde?
    Whilom thou was peregall to the best,
And wont to make the jolly shepeheards gladde,
    With pyping and dauncing did passe the rest.

*bestadde*, treated.

*Per.* Ah! Willye, now I have learnd a newe daunce;
My old musick mard by a newe mischaunce.

*Wil.* Mischiefe mought to that mischaunce befall,
  That so hath raft us of our meriment.
But reede me what payne doth thee so appall;
  Or lovest thou, or bene thy younglings miswent?
*Per.* Love hath misled both my younglings and mee:
I pyne for payne, and they my payne to see.

*Wil.* Perdie, and wellawaye, ill may they thrive!
  Never knew I lovers sheepe in good plight:
But, and if in rymes with me thou dare strive,
  Such fond fantsies shall soone be put to flight.
*Per.* That shall I doe, though mochell worse I fared:
Never shall be sayde that Perigot was dared.

*Wil.* Then loe, Perigot, the Pledge which I plight,
  A mazer ywrought of the Maple warre,
Wherein is enchased many a fayre sight
  Of Beres and Tygres, that maken fiers warre;
And over them spred a goodly wild vine,
Entrailed with a wanton Yvie twine.

Thereby is a Lambe in the Wolves jawes:
  But see, how fast renneth the shepheard swayne
To save the innocent from the beastes pawes,
  And here with his shepe-hooke hath him slayne.
Tell me, such a cup hast thou ever sene?
Well mought it beseme any harvest Queene.

*Per.* Thereto will I pawne yonder spotted Lambe,
  Of all my flocke there nis sike another,
For I brought him up without the Dambe:
  But Colin Clout rafte me of his brother,
That he purchast of me in the playne field:
Sore against my will was I forst to yield.

　　　　*mazer*, bowl.　　　　　*warre*, knot.

*Wil.* Sicker, make like account of his brother.
　But who shall judge the wager wonne or lost?
*Per.* That shall yonder heardgrome, and none other,
　Which over the pousse hetheward 'doth post.
*Wil.* But, for the Sunnbeame so sore doth us beate,
Were not better to shunne the scortching heate?

*Per.* Well agreed, Willie: then, sitte thee downe,
　　swayne:
　Sike a song never heardest thou but Colin sing.
*Cud.* Gynne when ye lyst, ye jolly shepheards twayne:
　Sike a judge as Cuddie were for a king.

*Per.* 'It fell upon a holy eve,
*Wil.* 　Hey, ho, hollidaye!
*Per.* When holy fathers wont to shrieve;
*Wil.* 　Now gynneth this roundelay.
*Per.* Sitting upon a hill so hye,
*Wil.* 　Hey, ho, the high hyll!
*Per.* The while my flocke did feede thereby;
*Wil.* 　The while the shepheard selfe did spill:
*Per.* I saw the bouncing Bellibone,
*Wil.* 　Hey, ho, Bonibell!
*Per.* Tripping over the dale alone,
*Wil.* 　She can trippe it very well:
*Per.* Well decked in a frocke of gray,
*Wil.* 　Hey, ho, gray is greete!
*Per.* And in a Kirtle of greene saye,
*Wil.* 　The greene is for maydens meete.
*Per.* A chapelet on her head she wore,
*Wil.* 　Hey, ho, chapelet!
*Per.* Of sweete Violets therein was store,
*Wil.* 　She sweeter then the Violet.
*Per.* My sheepe did leave theyr wonted food,

*Wil.*  Hey, ho, seely sheepe!
*Per.*  And gazd on her as they were wood,
*Wil.*  Woode as he that did them keepe.
*Per.*  As the bonilasse passed bye,
*Wil.*  Hey, ho, bonilasse!
*Per.*  She rovde at me with glauncing eye,
*Wil.*  As cleare as the christall glasse;
*Per.*  All as the Sunnye beame so bright,
*Wil.*  Hey, ho, the Sunne-beame!
*Per.*  Glaunceth from Phœbus face forthright.
*Wil.*  So love into thy hart did streame:
*Per.*  Or as the thonder cleaves the cloudes,
*Wil.*  Hey, ho, the Thonder!
*Per.*  Wherein the lightsome levin shroudes,
*Wil.*  So cleaves thy soule asonder:
*Per.*  Or as Dame Cynthias silver raye,
*Wil.*  Hey, ho, the Moonelight!
*Per.*  Upon the glyttering wave doth playe,
*Wil.*  Such play is a pitteous plight.
*Per.*  The glaunce into my heart did glide;
*Wil.*  Hey, ho, the glyder!
*Per.*  Therewith my soule was sharply gryde,
*Wil.*  Such woundes soone wexen wider.
*Per.*  Hasting to raunch the arrow out,
*Wil.*  Hey, ho, Perigot!
*Per.*  I left the head in my hart-roote,
*Wil.*  It was a desperate shot.
*Per.*  There it ranckleth, ay more and more,
*Wil.*  Hey, ho, the arrowe!
*Per.*  Ne can I find salve for my sore:
*Wil.*  Love is a curelesse sorrowe.
*Per.*  And though my bale with death I bought,
*Wil.*  Hey, ho, heavie cheere!

*Per.* Yet should thilk lasse not from my thought,
*Wil.*    So you may buye golde to deere.
*Per.* But whether in paynefull love I pyne,
*Wil.*    Hey, ho, pinching payne!
*Per.* Or thrive in welth, she shalbe mine,
*Wil.*    But if thou can her obteine.
*Per.* And if for gracelesse greefe I dye,
*Wil.*    Hey, ho, gracelesse griefe!
*Per.* Witnesse shee slewe me with her eye,
*Wil.*    Let thy follye be the priefe.
*Per.* And you, that sawe it, simple shepe,
*Wil.*    Hey, ho, the fayre flocke!
*Per.* For priefe thereof, my death shall weepe,
*Wil.*    And mone with many a mocke.
*Per.* So learnd I love on a holye eve,
*Wil.*    Hey, ho, holidaye!
*Per.* That ever since my hart did greve,
*Wil.*    Now endeth our roundelay.'

*Cud.* Sicker, sike a roundle never heard I none:
   Little lacketh Perigot of the best,
And Willye is not greatly overgone,
   So weren his under-songs well addrest.
*Wil.* Herdgrome, I fear me, thou have a squint eye:
Areede uprightly who has the victorye.

*Cud.* Fayth of my soule, I deeme ech have gayned:
   For-thy let the Lambe be Willye his owne:
And for Perigot, so well hath hym payned,
   To him be the wroughten mazer alone.

*Per.* Perigot is well pleased with the doome:
Ne can Willye wite the witelesse herdgroome.

*Wil.* Never dempt more right of beautye, I weene,
The shepheard of Ida that judged beauties Queene.

*Cud.* But tell me, shepherds, should it not yshend
  Your roundels fresh, to heare a doolefull verse
Of Rosalend (who knowes not Rosalend?)
  That Colin made? ylke can I you rehearse.
*Per.* Now say it, Cuddie, as thou art a ladde:
With mery thing its good to medle sadde.

*Wil.* Fayth of my soule, thou shalt ycrouned be
  In Colins stede, if thou this song areede;
For never thing on earth so pleaseth me
  As him to heare, or matter of his deede.
*Cud.* Then listneth ech unto my heavy laye,
And tune your pypes as ruthful as ye may.

'Ye wastefull Woodes! beare witnesse of my woe,
  Wherein my plaints did oftentimes resound:
  Ye carelesse byrds are privie to my cryes,
  Which in your songs were wont to make a part:
  Thou, pleasaunt spring, hast luld me oft asleepe,
  Whose streames my tricklinge teares did ofte aug-
    ment.
Resort of people doth my greefs augment,
  The walled townes doe worke my greater woe;
  The forest wide is fitter to resound
  The hollow Echo of my carefull cryes:
  I hate the house, since thence my love did part,
  Whose waylefull want debarres myne eyes from
    sleepe.
Let stremes of teares supply the place of sleepe;
  Let all, that sweete is, voyd: and all that may augment
  My doole, draw neare! More meete to wayle my woe
  Bene the wild woodes, my sorowes to resound,
  Then bedde, or bowre, both which I fill with cryes,
  When I them see so waist, and fynd no part

A. S.                                4

Of pleasure past.  Here will I dwell apart
  In gastfull grove therefore, till my last sleepe
  Doe close mine eyes: so shall I not augment
  With sight of such as chaunge my restlesse woe.
  Helpe me, ye banefull byrds, whose shrieking sound
  Ys signe of dreery death, my deadly cryes
Most ruthfully to tune: And as my cryes
  (Which of my woe cannot bewray least part)
  You heare all night, when nature craveth sleepe,
  Increase, so let your yrksome yells augment.
  Thus all the night in plaints, the daye in woe,
  I vowed have to wayst, till safe and sound
She home returne, whose voyces silver sound
  To cheerefull songs can chaunge my cherelesse cryes.
  Hence with the Nightingale will I take part,
  That blessed byrd, that spends her time of sleepe
  In songs and plaintive pleas, the more taugment
  The memory of hys misdeede that bred her woe.
And you that feele no woe, when as the sound
  Of these my nightly cryes ye heare apart,
  Let breake your sounder sleepe, and pitie augment.'

*Per*.  O Colin, Colin! the shepheards joye,
  How I admire ech turning of thy verse!
And Cuddie, fresh Cuddie, the liefest boye,
  How dolefully his doole thou didst rehearse!
*Cud*.  Then blowe your pypes, shepheards, til you be
     at home;
The night nigheth fast, yts time to be gone.

              *gastfull*, dreary.

## SEPTEMBER

ÆGLOGA NONA.    ARGUMENT

Herein Diggon Davie is devised to be a shepheard that,
in hope of more gayne, drove his sheepe into a farre
countrye. The abuses whereof, and loose living of
Popish prelates, by occasion of Hobbinols demaund,
he discourseth at large.

### HOBBINOL.  DIGGON DAVIE

*Hob.*  DIGGON DAVIE! I bidde her god day;
Or Diggon her is, or I missaye.
   *Dig.*  Her was her, while it was daye-light,
But now her is a most wretched wight:
For day, that was, is wightly past,
And now at earst the dirke night doth hast.
   *Hob.*  Diggon, areede who has thee so dight?
Never I wist thee in so poore a plight.
Where is the fayre flocke thou was wont to leade?
Or bene they chaffred, or at mischiefe dead?
   *Dig.*  Ah! for love of that is to thee moste leefe,
Hobbinol, I pray thee, gall not my old griefe:
Sike question ripeth up cause of newe woe,
For one, opened, mote unfolde many moe.
   *Hob.*  Nay, but sorrow close shrouded in hart,
I know, to kepe is a burdenous smart:
Eche thing imparted is more eath to beare:
When the rayne is faln, the cloudes wexen cleare.
And nowe, sithence I sawe thy head last,
Thrise three Moones bene fully spent and past;
Since when thou hast measured much grownd,
And wandred, I wene, about the world round,

    *wightly*, quickly.       *at earst*, at last.

So as thou can many thinges relate;
But tell me first of thy flocks estate.
   *Dig*. My sheepe bene wasted; (wae is me therefore!)
The jolly shepheard that was of yore
Is nowe nor jollye, nor shepeheard more.
In forrein costes men sayd was plentye;
And so there is, but all of miserye:
I dempt there much to have eeked my store,
But such eeking hath made my hart sore.
In tho countryes, whereas I have bene,
No being for those that truely mene;
But for such, as of guile maken gayne,
No such countrye as there to remaine;
They setten to sale their shops of shame,
And maken a Mart of theyr good name:
The shepheards there robben one another,
And layen baytes to beguile her brother;
Or they will buy his sheepe out of the cote,
Or they will carven the shepheards throte.
The shepheardes swayne you cannot wel ken,
But it be by his pryde, from other men:
They looken bigge as Bulls that bene bate,
And bearen the cragge so stiffe and so state,
As cocke on his dunghill crowing cranck.
   *Hob*. Diggon, I am so stiffe and so stanck,
That uneth may I stand any more:
And nowe the Westerne wind bloweth sore,
That nowe is in his chiefe sovereigntee,
Beating the withered leafe from the tree.
Sitte we downe here under the hill;
Tho may we talke and tellen our fill,
And make a mocke at the blustring blast.
Now say on, Diggon, what ever thou hast.

    *cranck*, vigorously.        *stanck*, wearily.

*Dig.* Hobbin, ah Hobbin! I curse the stounde
That ever I cast to have lorne this grounde:
Wel-away the while I was so fonde
To leave the good, that I had in hond,
In hope of better that was uncouth!
So lost the Dogge the flesh in his mouth.
My seely sheepe (ah, seely sheepe!)
That here by there I whilome usd to keepe,
All were they lustye as thou didst see,
Bene all sterved with pyne and penuree:
Hardly my selfe escaped thilke payne,
Driven for neede to come home agayne.

   *Hob.* Ah fon! now by thy losse art taught,
That seeldome chaunge the better brought:
Content who lives with tryed state
Neede feare no chaunge of frowning fate;
But who will seeke for unknowne gayne,
Oft lives by losse, and leaves with payne.

   *Dig.* I wote ne, Hobbin, how I was bewitcht
With vayne desire and hope to be enricht;
But, sicker, so it is, as the bright starre
Seemeth ay greater when it is farre:
I thought the soyle would have made me rich,
But nowe I wote it is nothing sich;
For eyther the shepheards bene ydle and still,
And ledde of theyr sheepe what way they wyll,
Or they bene false, and full of covetise,
And casten to compasse many wrong emprise:
But the more bene fraight with fraud and spight,
Ne in good nor goodnes taken delight,
But kindle coales of conteck and yre,
Wherewith they sette all the world on fire;
Which when they thinken agayne to quench,

       *stounde*, moment.

With holy water they doen hem all drench.
They saye they con to heaven the high-way,
But, by my soule, I dare undersaye
They never sette foote in that same troade,
But balk the right way, and strayen abroad.
They boast they han the devill at commaund,
But aske hem therefore what they han paund:
Marrie! that great Pan bought with deare borrow,
To quite it from the blacke bowre of sorrowe.
But they han sold thilk same long agoe,
For-thy woulden drawe with hem many moe.
But let hem gange alone a Gods name;
As they han brewed, so let hem beare blame.

   *Hob.* Diggon, I praye thee, speake not so dirke;
Such myster saying me seemeth to mirke.

   *Dig.* Then, playnely to speake of shepheards
      most what,
Badde is the best; (this English is flatt.)
Their ill haviour garres men missay
Both of their doctrine, and of theyr faye.
They sayne the world is much war then it wont,
All for her shepheards bene beastly and blont.
Other sayne, but how truely I note,
All for they holden shame of theyr cote:
Some sticke not to say, (whote cole on her tongue!)
That sike mischiefe graseth hem emong,
All for they casten too much of worlds care,
To deck her Dame, and enrich her heyre;
For such encheason, if you goe nye,
Fewe chymneis reeking you shall espye:
The fatte Oxe, that wont ligge in the stal,
Is nowe fast stalled in her crumenall.
Thus chatten the people in theyr steads,

*crumenall*, purse.

Ylike as a Monster of many heads;
But they that shooten neerest the pricke
Sayne, other the fat from their beards doen lick:
For bigge Bulles of Basan brace hem about,
That with theyr hornes butten the more stoute;
But the leane soules treaden under foote,
And to seeke redresse mought little boote;
For liker bene they to pluck away more,
Then ought of the gotten good to restore:
For they bene like foule wagmoires overgrast,
That, if thy galage once sticketh fast,
The more to wind it out thou doest swinck,
Thou mought ay deeper and deeper sinck.
Yet better leave of with a little losse,
Then by much wrestling to leese the grosse.
   *Hob.*  Nowe, Diggon, I see thou speakest to plaine;
Better it were a little to feyne,
And cleanly cover that cannot be cured:
Such ill, as is forced, mought nedes be endured.
But of sike pastoures howe done the flocks creepe?
   *Dig.*  Sike as the shepheards, sike bene her sheepe,
For they nill listen to the shepheards voyce,
But-if he call hem at theyr good choyce;
They wander at wil and stay at pleasure,
And to theyr foldes yeed at their owne leasure.
But they had be better come at their cal;
For many han into mischiefe fall,
And bene of ravenous Wolves yrent,
All for they nould be buxome and bent.
   *Hob.*  Fye on thee, Diggon, and all thy foule
     leasing!
Well is knowne that sith the Saxon king
Never was Woolfe seene, many nor some,

     *buxome and bent*, meek and obedient.

Nor in all Kent, nor in Christendome;
But the fewer Woolves (the soth to sayne)
The more bene the Foxes that here remaine.

   *Dig.* Yes, but they gang in more secrete wise,
And with sheepes clothing doen hem disguise.
They walke not widely as they were wont,
For feare of raungers and the great hunt,
But prively prolling to and froe,
Enaunter they mought be inly knowe.

   *Hob.* Or prive or pert yf any bene,
We han great Bandogs will teare their skinne.

   *Dig.* Indeede, thy Ball is a bold bigge curre,
And could make a jolly hole in theyr furre:
But not good Dogges hem needeth to chace,
But heedy shepheards to discerne their face;
For all their craft is in their countenaunce,
They bene so grave and full of mayntenaunce.
But shall I tell thee what my selfe knowe
Chaunced to Roffynn not long ygoe?

   *Hob.* Say it out, Diggon, whatever it hight,
For not but well mought him betight:
He is so meeke, wise, and merciable,
And with his word his worke is convenable.
Colin Clout, I wene, be his selfe boye,
(Ah, for Colin, he whilome my ioye!)
Shepheards sich, God mought us many send,
That doen so carefully theyr flocks tend.

   *Dig.* Thilk same shepheard mought I well marke,
He has a Dogge to byte or to barke;
Never had shepheard so kene a kurre,
That waketh and if but a leafe sturre.
Whilome there wonned a wicked Wolfe,
That with many a Lambe had glutted his gulfe,
And ever at night wont to repayre

Unto the flocke, when the Welkin shone faire,
Ycladde in clothing of seely sheepe,
When the good old man used to sleepe.
Tho at midnight he would barke and ball,
(For he had eft learned a curres call,)
As if a Woolfe were emong the sheepe:
With that the shepheard would breake his sleepe,
And send out Lowder (for so his dog hote)
To raunge the fields with wide open throte.
Tho, when as Lowder was farre awaye,
This Wolvish sheepe woulde catchen his pray,
A Lambe, or a Kidde, or a weanell wast;
With that to the wood would he speede him fast.
Long time he used this slippery pranck,
Ere Roffy could for his laboure him thanck.
At end, the shepheard his practise spyed,
(For Roffy is wise, and as Argus eyed,)
And when at even he came to the flocke,
Fast in theyr folds he did them locke,
And tooke out the Woolfe in his counterfect cote,
And let out the sheepes bloud at his throte.
  *Hob.* Marry, Diggon, what should him affraye
To take his owne where ever it laye?
For, had his wesand bene a little widder,
He would have devoured both hidder and shidder.
  *Dig.* Mischiefe light on him, and Gods great curse!
Too good for him had bene a great deale worse;
For it was a perilous beast above all,
And eke had he cond the shepherds call,
And oft in the night came to the shepe-cote,
And called Lowder, with a hollow throte,
As if it the old man selfe had bene:

> *weanell wast,* weaned youngling.
> *hidder and shidder,* male and female.

The dog his maisters voice did it wene,
Yet halfe in doubt he opened the dore,
And ranne out as he was wont of yore.
No sooner was out, but, swifter then thought,
Fast by the hyde the Wolfe Lowder caught;
And, had not Roffy renne to the steven,
Lowder had be slaine thilke same even.

    *Hob.*  God shield, man, he should so ill have thrive,
All for he did his devoyr belive!
If sike bene Wolves, as thou hast told,
How mought we, Diggon, hem be-hold?

    *Dig.*  How, but, with heede and watchfullnesse,
Forstallen hem of their wilinesse:
For-thy with shepheards sittes not playe,
Or sleepe, as some doen, all the long day;
But ever liggen in watch and ward,
From soddein force theyr flocks for to gard.

    *Hob.*  Ah, Diggon! thilke same rule were too straight,
All the cold season to wach and waite;
We bene of fleshe, men as other bee,
Why should we be bound to such miseree?
Whatever thing lacketh chaungeable rest,
Mought needes decay, when it is at best.

    *Dig.*  Ah! but, Hobbinoll, all this long tale
Nought easeth the care that doth me forhaile;
What shall I doe? what way shall I wend,
My piteous plight and losse to amend?
Ah! good Hobbinoll, mought I thee praye
Of ayde or counsell in my decaye.

    *Hob.*  Now, by my soule, Diggon, I lament
The haplesse mischiefe that has thee hent;
Nethelesse thou seest my lowly saile,

        *steven*, noise.    *belive*, quickly.    *forhaile*, distress.

That froward fortune doth ever availe:
But, were Hobbinoll as God mought please,
Diggon should soone find favour and ease:
But if to my cotage thou wilt resort,
So as I can I wil thee comfort;
There mayst thou ligge in a vetchy bed,
Till fayrer Fortune shewe forth her head.

 *Dig.* Ah, Hobbinoll! God mought it thee requite;
Diggon on fewe such freends did ever lite.


## OCTOBER

### ÆGLOGA DECIMA. ARGUMENT

In Cuddie is set out the perfecte paterne of a Poete
whiche, finding no maintenaunce of his state and studies,
complayneth of the contempte of Poetrie, and the
causes thereof: Specially having bene in all ages, and
even amongst the most barbarous, alwayes of singular
accoumpt and honor, and being indede so worthy and
commendable an arte; or rather no arte, but a divine
gift and heavenly instinct not to bee gotten by laboure
and learning, but adorned with both; and poured into
the witte by a certain Ἐνθουσιασμὸς and celestiall
inspiration, as the Author hereof els where at large
discourseth in his booke called *The English Poete*, which
booke being lately come to my hands, I mynde also by
Gods grace, upon further advisement, to publish.

### PIERCE. CUDDIE

 *Piers.* CUDDIE, for shame! hold up thy heavye head,
And let us cast with what delight to chace,
And weary thys long lingring Phœbus race.
Whilome thou wont the shepheards laddes to leade
In rymes, in ridles, and in bydding base;
Now they in thee, and thou in sleepe art dead.

*Cud.* Piers, I have pyped erst so long with payne,
That all mine Oten reedes bene rent and wore,
And my poore Muse hath spent her spared store,
Yet little good hath got, and much lesse gayne.
Such pleasaunce makes the Grashopper so poore,
And ligge so layd, when Winter doth her straine.

The dapper ditties, that I wont devise
To feede youthes fancie, and the flocking fry,
Delighten much; what I the bett for-thy?
They han the pleasure, I a sclender prise;
I beate the bush, the byrds to them doe flye:
What good thereof to Cuddie can arise?

*Piers.* Cuddie, the prayse is better then the price,
The glory eke much greater then the gayne:
O! what an honor is it, to restraine
The lust of lawlesse youth with good advice,
Or pricke them forth with pleasaunce of thy vaine,
Whereto thou list their trayned willes entice.

Soone as thou gynst to sette thy notes in frame,
O, how the rurall routes to thee doe cleave!
Seemeth thou dost their soule of sence bereave;
All as the shepheard that did fetch his dame
From Plutoes balefull bowre withouten leave,
His musicks might the hellish hound did tame.

*Cud.* So praysen babes the Peacoks spotted traine,
And wondren at bright Argus blazing eye;
But who rewards him ere the more for-thy,
Or feedes him once the fuller by a graine?
Sike prayse is smoke, that sheddeth in the skye;
Sike words bene wynd, and wasten soone in vayne.

*layd*, faint.

*Piers.*  Abandon, then, the base and viler clowne;
Lyft up thy selfe out of the lowly dust,
And sing of bloody Mars, of wars, of giusts;
Turne thee to those that weld the awful crowne,
To doubted Knights, whose woundlesse armour rusts,
And helmes unbruzed wexen dayly browne.

There may thy Muse display her fluttryng wing,
And stretch her selfe at large from East to West;
Whither thou list in fayre Elisa rest,
Or, if thee please in bigger notes to sing,
Advaunce the worthy whome shee loveth best,
That first the white beare to the stake did bring.

And, when the stubborne stroke of stronger stounds
Has somewhat slackt the tenor of thy string,
Of love and lustihead tho mayst thou sing,
And carroll lowde, and leade the Myllers rownde,
All were Elisa one of thilke same ring;
So mought our Cuddies name to heaven sownde.

*Cud.*  Indeede the Romish Tityrus, I heare,
Through his Mecænas left his Oaten reede,
Whereon he earst had taught his flocks to feede,
And laboured lands to yield the timely eare,
And eft did sing of warres and deadly drede,
So as the Heavens did quake his verse to here.

But ah! Mecænas is yclad in claye,
And great Augustus long ygoe is dead,
And all the worthies liggen wrapt in leade,
That matter made for Poets on to play:
For ever, who in derring-doe were dreade,
The loftie verse of hem was loved aye.

But after vertue gan for age to stoope,
And mightie manhode brought a bedde of ease,
The vaunting Poets found nought worth a pease
To put in preace emong the learned troupe:
Tho gan the streames of flowing wittes to cease,
And sonne-bright honour pend in shamefull coupe.

And if that any buddes of Poesie,
Yet of the old stocke, gan to shoote agayne,
Or it mens follies mote be forst to fayne,
And rolle with rest in rymes of rybaudrye;
Or, as it sprong, it wither must agayne:
Tom Piper makes us better melodie.

*Piers.*  O pierlesse Poesye! where is then thy place?
If nor in Princes pallace thou doe sitt,
(And yet is Princes pallace the most fitt,)
Ne brest of baser birth doth thee embrace,
Then make thee winges of thine aspyring wit,
And, whence thou camst, flye backe to heaven apace.

*Cud.*  Ah, Percy! it is all to weake and wanne,
So high to sore and make so large a flight;
Her peeced pyneons bene not so in plight:
For Colin fittes such famous flight to scanne;
He, were he not with love so ill bedight,
Would mount as high, and sing as soote as Swanne.

*Piers.*  Ah, fon! for love does teach him climbe so
     hie,
And lyftes him up out of the loathsome myre:
Such immortal mirrhor, as he doth admire,
Would rayse ones mynd above the starry skie,
And cause a caytive corage to aspire;
For lofty love doth loath a lowly eye.

*Cud.* All otherwise the state of Poet stands;
For lordly love is such a Tyranne fell,
That where he rules all power he doth expell;
The vaunted verse a vacant head demaundes,
Ne wont with crabbed care the Muses dwell:
Unwisely weaves, that takes two webbes in hand.

Who ever casts to compasse weightye prise,
And thinkes to throwe out thondring words of threate,
Let powre in lavish cups and thriftie bitts of meate,
For Bacchus fruite is frend to Phœbus wise;
And, when with Wine the braine begins to sweate,
The nombers flowe as fast as spring doth ryse.

Thou kenst not, Percie, howe the ryme should rage,
O! if my temples were distaind with wine,
And girt in girlonds of wild Yvie twine,
How I could reare the Muse on stately stage,
And teache her tread aloft in buskin fine,
With queint Bellona in her equipage!

But ah! my corage cooles ere it be warme:
For-thy content us in thys humble shade,
Where no such troublous tydes han us assayde;
Here we our slender pypes may safely charme.
  *Piers.* And, when my Gates shall han their bellies
          layd,
Cuddie shall have a Kidde to store his farme.


## NOVEMBER

### ÆGLOGA UNDECIMA.   ARGUMENT

In this xi. Æglogue hee bewayleth the death of some
mayden of great bloud, whom he calleth Dido. The
personage is secrete, and to me altogether unknowne,

albe of him selfe I often required the same. This
Æglogue is made in imitation of Marot his song, which
he made upon the death of Loys the Frenche Queene;
but farre passing his reache, and in myne opinion all
other the Eglogues of this booke.

THENOT. COLIN

*The.* COLIN, my deare, when shall it please thee sing,
As thou were wont, songs of some jouisaunce?
Thy Muse to long slombreth in sorrowing,
Lulled a sleepe through loves misgovernaunce.
Now somewhat sing, whose endles sovenaunce
Emong the shepeheards swaines may aye remaine,
Whether thee list thy loved lasse advaunce,
Or honor Pan with hymnes of higher vaine.

*Col.* Thenot, now nis the time of merimake,
Nor Pan to herye, nor with love to playe;
Sike myrth in May is meetest for to make,
Or summer shade, under the cocked hay.
But nowe sadde Winter welked hath the day,
And Phœbus, weary of his yerely taske,
Ystabled hath his steedes in lowlye laye,
And taken up his ynne in Fishes haske.
Thilke sollein season sadder plight doth aske,
And loatheth sike delightes as thou doest prayse:
The mornefull Muse in myrth now list ne maske,
As shee was wont in youngth and sommer dayes;
But if thou algate lust light virelayes,
And looser songs of love to underfong,
Who but thy selfe deserves sike Poetes prayse?
Relieve thy Oaten pypes that sleepen long.

*The.* The Nightingale is sovereigne of song,
Before him sits the Titmose silent bee;

welked, shortened.          haske, basket.

And I, unfitte to thrust in skilfull thronge,
Should Colin make judge of my fooleree:
Nay, better learne of hem that learned bee,
And han be watered at the Muses well;
The kindelye dewe drops from the higher tree,
And wets the little plants that lowly dwell.
But if sadde winters wrathe, and season chill,
Accorde not with thy Muses meriment,
To sadder times thou mayst attune thy quill,
And sing of sorrowe and deathes dreeriment;
For deade is Dido, dead, alas! and drent;
Dido! the greate shepehearde his daughter sheene.
The fayrest May she was that ever went,
Her like shee has not left behinde I weene:
And, if thou wilt bewayle my wofull tene,
I shall thee give yond Cosset for thy payne;
And, if thy rymes as rownde and rufull bene
As those that did thy Rosalind complayne,
Much greater gyfts for guerdon thou shalt gayne,
Then Kidde or Cosset, which I thee bynempt.
Then up, I say, thou jolly shepeheard swayne,
Let not my small demaund be so contempt.

  *Col.*  Thenot, to that I choose thou doest me tempt;
But ah! to well I wote my humble vaine,
And howe my rimes bene rugged and unkempt;
Yet, as I conne, my conning I will strayne.

'Up, then, Melpomene! the mournefulst Muse of nyne,
Such cause of mourning never hadst afore;
Up, grieslie ghostes! and up my rufull ryme!
Matter of myrth now shalt thou have no more;
For dead shee is, that myrth thee made of yore.

*drent*, drowned.    *Cosset*, lamb brought up without the dam.

Dido, my deare, alas! is dead,
Dead, and lyeth wrapt in lead.
O heavie herse!
Let streaming teares be poured out in store;
O carefull verse!

'Shepheards, that by your flocks on Kentish downes
          abyde,
Waile ye this wofull waste of Natures warke;
Waile we the wight whose presence was our pryde;
Waile we the wight whose absence is our carke;
The sonne of all the world is dimme and darke:
    The earth now lacks her wonted light,
    And all we dwell in deadly night.
    O heavie herse!
Breake we our pypes, that shrild as lowde as Larke;
    O carefull verse!

'Why doe we longer live, (ah! why live we so long?)
Whose better dayes death hath shut up in woe?
The fayrest floure our gyrlond all emong
Is faded quite, and into dust ygoe.
Sing now, ye shepheards daughters, sing no moe
    The songs that Colin made you in her praise,
    But into weeping turne your wanton layes.
    O heavie herse!
Nowe is time to dye: Nay, time was long ygoe:
    O carefull verse!

'Whence is it, that the flouret of the field doth fade,
And lyeth buryed long in Winters bale;
Yet, soone as spring his mantle hath displayde,
It floureth fresh, as it should never fayle?
But thing on earth that is of most availe,

As vertues braunch and beauties budde,
Reliven not for any good.
    O heavie herse!
The braunch once dead, the budde eke needes must quaile;
    O carefull verse!

'She, while she was, (that was, a woful word to sayne!)
For beauties prayse and plesaunce had no peere;
So well she couth the shepherds entertayne
With cakes and cracknells, and such country chere:
Ne would she scorne the simple shepheards swaine;
    For she would cal him often heame,
    And give him curds and clouted Creame.
    O heavie herse!
Als Colin Cloute she would not once disdayne;
    O carefull verse!

'But nowe sike happy cheere is turnd to heavie chaunce,
Such pleasaunce now displast by dolors dint:
All musick sleepes, where death doth leade the daunce,
And shepherds wonted solace is extinct.
The blew in black, the greene in gray is tinct;
    The gaudie girlonds deck her grave,
    The faded flowres her corse embrave.
    O heavie herse!
Morne nowe, my Muse, now morne with teares besprint;
    O carefull verse!

'O thou greate shepheard, Lobbin, how great is thy
        griefe!
Where bene the nosegayes that she dight for thee?
The coloured chaplets wrought with a chiefe,
The knotted rush-ringes, and gilte Rosemaree?
            *with a chiefe*, into a nosegay.

For shee deemed nothing too deere for thee.
　Ah! they bene all yclad in clay;
　One bitter blast blewe all away.
　O heavie herse!
Thereof nought remaynes but the memoree;
　O carefull verse!

'Ay me! that dreerie Death should strike so mortall
　　　stroke,
That can undoe Dame Natures kindly course;
The faded lockes fall from the loftie oke,
The flouds do gaspe, for dryed is theyr sourse,
And flouds of teares flowe in theyr stead perforse:
　The mantled medowes mourne,
　Theyr sondry colours tourne.
　O heavie herse!
The heavens doe melt in teares without remorse;
　O carefull verse!

'The feeble flocks in field refuse their former foode,
And hang theyr heads as they would learne to weepe;
The beastes in forest wayle as they were woode,
Except the Wolves, that chase the wandring sheepe,
Now she is gone that safely did hem keepe:
　The Turtle on the bared braunch
　Laments the wound that death did launch.
　O heavie herse!
And Philomele her song with teares doth steepe;
　O carefull verse!

'The water Nymphs, that wont with her to sing and
　　　daunce,
And for her girlond Olive braunches beare,
Nowe balefull boughes of Cypres doen advaunce;
The Muses, that were wont greene bayes to weare,

Now bringen bitter Eldre braunches seare;
   The fatall sisters eke repent
   Her vitall threde so soone was spent.
   O heavie herse!
Morne now, my Muse, now morne with heavy cheare,
   O carefull verse!

'O! trustlesse state of earthly things, and slipper hope
Of mortal men, that swincke and sweate for nought,
And, shooting wide, doe misse the marked scope;
Now have I learnd (a lesson derely bought)
That nys on earth assuraunce to be sought;
   For what might be in earthlie mould,
   That did her buried body hould.
   O heavie herse!
Yet saw I on the beare when it was brought;
   O carefull verse!

'But maugre death, and dreaded sisters deadly spight,
And gates of hel, and fyrie furies forse,
She hath the bonds broke of eternall night,
Her soule unbodied of the burdenous corpse.
Why then weepes Lobbin so without remorse?
   O Lobb! thy losse no longer lament;
   Dido nis dead, but into heaven hent.
   O happye herse!
Cease now, my Muse, now cease thy sorrowes sourse;
   O joyfull verse!

'Why wayle we then? why weary we the Gods with
       playnts,
As if some evill were to her betight?
She raignes a goddesse now emong the saintes,
That whilome was the saynt of shepheards light,
And is enstalled nowe in heavens hight.

I see thee, blessed soule, I see
Walke in Elisian fieldes so free.
    O happy herse!
Might I once come to thee, (O that I might!)
    O joyfull verse!

'Unwise and wretched men, to weete whats good or ill,
We deeme of Death as doome of ill desert;
But knewe we, fooles, what it us bringes until,
Dye would we dayly, once it to expert!
No daunger there the shepheard can astert;
    Fayre fieldes and pleasaunt layes there bene;
    The fieldes ay fresh, the grasse ay greene.
    O happy herse!
Make hast, ye shepheards, thether to revert:
    O joyfull verse!

'Dido is gone afore; (whose turne shall be the next?)
There lives shee with the blessed Gods in blisse,
There drincks she Nectar with Ambrosia mixt,
And joyes enjoyes that mortall men doe misse.
The honor now of highest gods she is,
    That whilome was poore shepheards pryde,
    While here on earth she did abyde.
    O happy herse!
Ceasse now, my song, my woe now wasted is;
    O joyfull verse!'

    *The*. Ay, francke shepheard, how bene thy verses
        meint
With doleful pleasaunce, so as I ne wotte
Whether rejoyce or weepe for great constrainte.
Thyne be the cossette, well hast thow it gotte.
Up, Colin up! ynough thou morned hast;
Now gynnes to mizzle, hye we homeward fast.

## DECEMBER

### ÆGLOGA DUODECIMA.   ARGUMENT

This Æglogue (even as the first beganne) is ended with
a complaynte of Colin to God Pan; wherein, as weary
of his former wayes, hee proportioneth his life to the
foure seasons of the yeare; comparing hys youthe to
the spring time, when he was fresh and free from loves
follye. His manhoode to the sommer, which, he sayth,
was consumed with greate heate and excessive drouth,
caused throughe a Comet or blasing starre, by which
hee meaneth love; which passion is commonly compared to such flames and immoderate heate. His riper
yeares hee resembleth to an unseasonable harveste,
wherein the fruites fall ere they be rype. His latter
age to winters chyll and frostie season, now drawing
neare to his last ende.

The gentle shepheard satte beside a springe,
All in the shadowe of a bushye brere,
That Colin hight, which wel could pype and singe,
For he of Tityrus his songs did lere:
    There, as he satte in secreate shade alone,
    Thus gan he make of love his piteous mone.

'O soveraigne Pan! thou god of shepheards all,
Which of our tender Lambkins takest keepe,
And, when our flocks into mischaunce mought fall,
Doest save from mischiefe the unwary sheepe,
    Als of their maisters hast no lesse regarde
    Then of the flocks, which thou doest watch and warde;

'I thee beseche (so be thou deigne to heare
Rude ditties, tund to shepheards Oaten reede,
Or if I ever sonet song so cleare,
As it with pleasaunce mought thy fancie feede)
    Hearken awhile, from thy greene cabinet,
    The rurall song of carefull Colinet.

'Whilome in youth, when flowrd my joyfull spring,
Like Swallow swift I wandred here and there;
For heate of heedlesse lust me so did sting,
That I of doubted daunger had no feare:
  I went the wastefull woodes and forest wide,
  Withouten dreade of Wolves to bene espyed.

'I wont to raunge amydde the mazie thickette,
And gather nuttes to make me Christmas game,
And joyed oft to chace the trembling Pricket,
Or hunt the hartlesse hare til shee were tame.
  What recked I of wintrye ages waste?—
  Tho deemed I my spring would ever laste.

'How often have I scaled the craggie Oke,
All to dislodge the Raven of her nest?
How have I wearied with many a stroke
The stately Walnut-tree, the while the rest
  Under the tree fell all for nuts at strife?
  For ylike to me was libertee and lyfe.

'And for I was in thilke same looser yeares,
(Whether the Muse so wrought me from my byrth,
Or I to much beleeved my shepherd peeres,)
Somedele ybent to song and musicks mirth,
  A good old shephearde, Wrenock was his name,
  Made me by arte more cunning in the same.

'Fro thence I durst in derring-doe compare
With shepheards swayne what ever fedde in field;
And, if that Hobbinol right judgement bare,
To Pan his owne selfe pype I neede not yield:
  For, if the flocking Nymphes did folow Pan,
  The wiser Muses after Colin ranne.

'But, ah! such pryde at length was ill repayde:
The shepheards God (perdie God was he none)
My hurtlesse pleasaunce did me ill upbraide;
My freedome lorne, my life he lefte to mone.
  Love they him called that gave me checkmate,
  But better mought they have behote him Hate.

'Tho gan my lovely Spring bid me farewel,
And Sommer season sped him to display
(For love then in the Lyons house did dwell)
The raging fyre that kindled at his ray.
  A comett stird up that unkindly heate,
  That reigned (as men sayd) in Venus seate.

'Forth was I ledde, not as I wont afore,
When choise I had to choose my wandring waye,
But whether luck and loves unbridled lore
Woulde leade me forth on Fancies bitte to playe:
  The bush my bedde, the bramble was my bowre,
  The Woodes can witnesse many a wofull stowre.

'Where I was wont to seeke the honey Bee,
Working her formall rowmes in wexen frame,
The grieslie Tode-stoole growne there mought I se,
And loathed Paddocks lording on the same:
  And where the chaunting birds luld me asleepe,
  The ghastlie Owle her grievous ynne doth keepe.

'Then as the springe gives place to elder time,
And bringeth forth the fruite of sommers pryde;
Also my age, now passed youngthly pryme,
To thinges of ryper season selfe applyed,
  And learnd of lighter timber cotes to frame,
  Such as might save my sheepe and me fro shame.

'To make fine cages for the Nightingale,
And Baskets of bulrushes, was my wont:
Who to entrappe the fish in winding sale
Was better seene, or hurtful beastes to hont?
    I learned als the signes of heaven to ken,
    How Phœbe fayles, where Venus sittes, and when.

'And tryed time yet taught me greater thinges;
The sodain rysing of the raging seas,
The soothe of byrdes by beating of their winges,
The power of herbs, both which can hurt and ease,
    And which be wont t' enrage the restlesse sheepe,
    And which be wont to worke eternall sleepe.

'But, ah! unwise and witlesse Colin Cloute,
That kydst the hidden kinds of many a wede,
Yet kydst not ene to cure thy sore hart-roote,
Whose ranckling wound as yet does rifelye bleede.
    Why livest thou stil, and yet hast thy deathes
        wound?
    Why dyest thou stil, and yet alive art founde?

'Thus is my sommer worne away and wasted,
Thus is my harvest hastened all to ræthe;
The eare that budded faire is burnt and blasted,
And all my hoped gaine is turnd to scathe:
    Of all the seede that in my youth was sowne
    Was nought but brakes and brambles to be mowne.

'My boughes with bloosmes that crowned were at firste,
And promised of timely fruite such store,
Are left both bare and barrein now at erst;
The flattring fruite is fallen to grownd before,
    And rotted ere they were halfe mellow ripe;
    My harvest wast, my hope away dyd wipe.

        *sale*, sallow.        *kydst*, knewest.

'The fragrant flowres, that in my garden grewe,
Bene withered, as they had bene gathered long;
Theyr rootes bene dryed up for lacke of dewe,
Yet dewed with teares they han be ever among.
  Ah! who has wrought my Rosalind this spight,
  To spil the flowres that should her girlond dight?

'And I, that whilome wont to frame my pype
Unto the shifting of the shepheards foote,
Sike follies nowe have gathered as too ripe,
And cast hem out as rotten and unsoote.
  The loser Lasse I cast to please no more;
  One if I please, enough is me therefore.

'And thus of all my harvest-hope I have
Nought reaped but a weedye crop of care;
Which, when I thought have thresht in swelling sheave,
Cockel for corne, and chaffe for barley, bare:
  Soone as the chaffe should in the fan be fynd,
  All was blowne away of the wavering wynd.

'So now my yeare drawes to his latter terme,
My spring is spent, my sommer burnt up quite;
My harveste hasts to stirre up Winter sterne,
And bids him clayme with rigorous rage hys right:
  So nowe he stormes with many a sturdy stoure;
  So now his blustring blast eche coste dooth scoure.

'The carefull cold hath nypt my rugged rynde,
And in my face deepe furrowes eld hath pight:
My head besprent with hoary frost I fynd,
And by myne eie the Crow his clawe dooth wright:
  Delight is layd abedde; and pleasure past;
  No sonne now shines; cloudes han all overcast.

'Now leave, ye shepheards boyes, your merry glee;
My Muse is hoarse and wearie of thys stounde:
Here will I hang my pype upon this tree:
Was never pype of reede did better sounde.
  Winter is come that blowes the bitter blaste,
  And after Winter dreerie death does hast.

'Gather together ye my little flocke,
My little flock, that was to me so liefe;
Let me, ah! lette me in your foldes ye lock,
Ere the breme Winter breede you greater griefe.
  Winter is come, that blowes the balefull breath,
  And after Winter commeth timely death.

'Adieu, delightes, that lulled me asleepe;
Adieu, my deare, whose love I bought so deare;
Adieu, my little Lambes and loved sheepe;
Adieu, ye Woodes, that oft my witnesse were:
  Adieu, good Hobbinoll, that was so true,
  Tell Rosalind, her Colin bids her adieu.'


  *Loe! I have made a Calender for every yeare,*
  *That steele in strength, and time in durance, shall outweare;*
  *And, if I marked well the starres revolution,*
  *It shall continewe till the worlds dissolution,*
  *To teach the ruder shepheard how to feede his sheepe,*
  *And from the falsers fraude his folded flocke to keepe.*

  *Goe, lyttle Calender! thou hast a free passeporte;*
  *Goe but a lowly gate emongste the meaner sorte:*
  *Dare not to match thy pype with Tityrus his style,*
  *Nor with the Pilgrim that the Ploughman playde awhyle;*
  *But followe them farre off, and their high steppes adore:*
  *The better please, the worse despise; I aske no more.*